DISCOVERING THE PAST TH

ARCHAEOLOGY

DISCOVERING THE PAST THROUGH
ARCHAEOLOGY

How to study an excavation: a practical book for the amateur archaeologist, with more than 300 photographs, maps and detailed illustrations

CHRISTOPHER CATLING

CONSULTANT: FIONA HAUGHEY

southwater

PICTURE ACKNOWLEDGEMENTS
(b: bottom, l: left, m: middle, r: right, t: top).
Anness Publishing Ltd would like to thank the following people for location photography:
Wiggold Summer School, Abbey Home Farm, Cirencester, UK, to Will and Hilary Chester-Master at Abbey Home Farm and Professor Timothy Darvill at the School of Conservation Sciences, University of Bournemouth, UK, and **Berkeley Castle Summer School,** Berkeley, Gloucestershire, UK, to Dr Stuart Prior and Dr Mark Horton of the Department of Archaeology and Anthropology, University of Bristol, UK, in conjunction with the Berkeley Castle Charitable Trust, for granting permission to photograph these ongoing archaeological projects. Thanks also to the students of the School of Conservation Sciences and those who attended the summer school, many of whom feature in the photographs; **Bristol Harbourside Excavation,** thanks to Jim Dyer of Crest Nicholson South West Ltd, Bristol, for granting permission to photograph the excavation, and to the employees of Wessex Archaeology (www.wessexarch.co.uk) for featuring in the photographs. The following photographs are ©**Anness Publishing Ltd** 24t, 26bl, 26br, 44t, 58bl, 93l, 94t, 98bl, 100bl, 102br, 117l, 121t **Anthony Duke (based on original drawings by Fiona Haughey)** ©**Anness Publishing Ltd** 12b, 18bl **Anthony Duke** ©**Anness Publishing Ltd** 27t, 30b, 61t, 63b, 65b **APVA Preservation Virginia** 124t, 124m, 124bl, 124br, 125bl, 125br **Blombos Caves Project** 64t **Bob Reece, Friends of Little Bighorn** 106br, 107l, 107m, 107r **Bridgeman Art Library** 76bl ©**Buckinghamshire County Council** 29b **Çatalhöyük Research Project** 90t, 90bl, 90br, 91tr, 91tl **Clive Ruggles** 113b **Corbis** 15tr, 16b, 17bl, 18br, 19b, 19tr, 21t, 23m, 23t, 25b, 27b, 28b, 30t, 32br, 32t, 32bl, 34t, 34b, 35t, 37bl, 38br, 39t, 39b, 42t, 46t, 47b, 47tl, 47tr, 52, 54br, 54bl, 54t, 55b, 55t, 56br, 56bl, 57b, 58t, 59t, 62t, 62br, 64br, 65t, 66t, 66b, 67b, 70br, 70bl, 74t, 75b, 77tr, 77b, 79tl, 82bm, 82t, 83br, 84t, 85bl, 87tl 96bl, 96br, 99t, 102bl, 103t, 103bl, 104bl, 108t, 108bl, 108br, 109bl, 109br, 111tl, 111tr, 111b, 112bl, 112br, 113tr, 113tl, 118t, 119tl, 122bl, 123tr, 123b, **The Daily Telegraph** 67tr **Dani Nadel** 71tr, 71tl, 71br **Den Y Ovenden** ©**Anness Publishing Ltd** 60b **Dr Susan O'Connor, Research School of Pacific and Asian Studies, Australian National University, Canberra** 63t **The Flag Fen Bronze Age Centre** /John Byford and Mike Webber 74b, 76t **George Willcox** 72t, 72br, 72bl, 73b **Getty Images** 8, 9m, 10b, 14bl, 16t, 28t, 31b, 37tl, 38bl, 45t, 57m, 62bl, 88br, 89b, 92, 93m, 93r, 104t, 105b, 105tr, 105tl **Göran Burenhult** 46br, 64bl ©**iStockphoto.com** 79tr, 82bl, 87b, 95t, 106bl, 110br / Andy Pritchard 75tl / cenap refik ONGAN 118bl / Christina Hanck 119tr / Claudio Giovanni Colombo 98bl / David Pedre 78bl / Diana Bier 82br / Fabio Bianchini 80br / hazel proudlove 73tl / Hedda Gjerpen 122t / Jamo Gonzalez Zarraonandia 89t / Jan Rihak 110t / Javier Garcia Blanco 76br / John Brennan 73tr / John Leigh 99b / Joseph Justice 117m / Leslie Banks 78t / luca manieri 109t / Luis Seco 88t / Mark Scott 88bm / Mary Lane 101l / Matt Trommer 75tr / Merijn van der Vliet 120b / Michael Fuery 79b / Natalia Bratslavsky 74m / Neil Sorenson 80t / Oleksiy Kondratyuk 95b / Paul Kline 80bl / Robert Bremec 85tr, 98t / Roberto A Sanchez / Simon Podgorsek 81 / Steve Geer 94bl, 94br / Steven Allan 88bl / Steven Phraner 101r / Tan Kian Khoon 86t / Volkan Ersoy 78br / Wojciech Zwierzynski 86b / **Jonathon Tubb** 43b / **Jonathan Reif** 71bl **The Landmarks Trust** 114bl, 114br, 114t, 115bm, 115br, 115bl, 115tr **The Mary Rose Trust** 96t, 97tr ©**Musuem of London** 48t / Derek Lucas 48br **Musuem of London Archaeology Service** 17t, 48bl, 49b, 97tl / Andy Chopping 9l, 10t, 11tl, 13t, 25tr, 48bm, 83t, / Jan Scrivener 38t / Jon Bailey 24b ©**Oxford Archaeology North** 33b / MLA 15tm **The Oxford Archaeological Unit Ltd** 9r, 12t, 13b, 15tl, 15bl, 15br 26t, 99m, 102t, 106bm, 106t, 118br **Peter Drewett** 31t, 31m **Professor Vince Gaffney, Institute of Archaeology and Antiquity** 68b **Scarborough Museums Trust** 67tl **Science Museum/Science and Society Picture Library** 41b **Science Photo Library** 18t, 20t, 21bl, 21br, 22b, 22t, 23b, 35b, 42b, 46bl, 56t, 57t, 58br, 59bl, 59br, 60t, 61b, 103br **Sheffield City Archives** 16ml, 16mr **Stuart Bedford** 45m, 45b, 87tr **Sturt W Manning, Aegean Dendrochronology Project** 50t, 50b, 51t, 51bl, 51br **Wessex Archaeology** 11tr, 11br, 14t, 14br, 17br, 20b, 25tl, 29r, 29tl, 37tr, 37br, 40bl, 44bl, 44br, 68t, 69t, 69b,100t, 100br, 116, 117r, 120t, 121b, 123tl **Werner Forman Archive** 36t, 36b, 40t, 40br, 41t, 43t, 77m, 85br

This edition is published by Southwater,
an imprint of Anness Publishing Ltd,
Blaby Road, Wigston, Leicestershire LE18 4SE

info@anness.com

www.southwaterbooks.com; www.annesspublishing.com

If you like the images in this book and would like to investigate using them for publishing, promotions or advertising, please visit our website www.practicalpictures.com for more information.

Publisher: Joanna Lorenz
Editorial Director: Helen Sudell
Project Editor: Melanie Hibbert
Production Controller: Bessie Bai
Photographers: Robert Pickett and Mark Wood
Book Design: Ian Sandom
Jacket Design: Nigel Partridge

ETHICAL TRADING POLICY
At Anness Publishing we believe that business should be conducted in an ethical and ecologically sustainable way, with respect for the environment and a proper regard to the replacement of the natural resources we employ. As a publisher, we use a lot of wood pulp in high-quality paper for printing, and that wood commonly comes from spruce trees. We are therefore currently growing more than 750,000 trees in three Scottish forest plantations: Berrymoss (130 hectares/320 acres), West Touxhill (125 hectares/305 acres) and Deveron Forest (75 hectares/185 acres). The forests we manage contain more than 3.5 times the number of trees employed each year in making paper for the books we manufacture. Because of this ongoing ecological investment programme, you, as our customer, can have the pleasure and reassurance of knowing that a tree is being cultivated on your behalf to naturally replace the materials used to make the book you are holding.
Our forestry programme is run in accordance with the UK Woodland Assurance Scheme (UKWAS) and will be certified by the internationally recognized Forest Stewardship Council (FSC). The FSC is a non-government organization dedicated to promoting responsible management of the world's forests. Certification ensures forests are managed in an environmentally sustainable and socially responsible way. For further information about this scheme, go to www.annesspublishing.com/trees

A CIP catalogue record for this book is available from the British Library.

PUBLISHER'S NOTE
Although the advice and information in this book are believed to be accurate and true at the time of going to press, neither the authors nor the publisher can accept any legal responsiblity or liability for any errors or omissions that may be made, nor for any inaccuracies nor for any loss, harm or injury that comes about from following instructions or advice in this book.

CONTENTS

Introduction   6

Studying the Finds   **8**
Beginning the Post-Excavation Process   10
Creating a Chronological Framework   12
Using Artefacts as Dating Evidence   14
Earliest and Latest Dates   16
Radiocarbon Dating   18
Selecting Samples for Carbon Dating   20
Advanced Dating Strategies   22
Dendrochronology and Other Dating Methods   24
Finds and Typologies   26
Building Typologies   28
Seriation and Trends   30
Ancient Environments   32
The Human Response to Climate Change   34
Metalwork Finds   36
Pottery as Evidence of Everyday Life   38
Pottery: the Key to Food Preparation   40
Ancient Diets   42
Analysing Human Remains   44
The Information in our Genes   46
Preparing the Publication and the Archive   48
Case Study: the Aegean
   Dendrochronology Project   50

Chronologies   **52**
Defining the Ages   54
The Earliest Humas   56
The Palaeolithic Era   58
Populating the World   60
Caves and Colonization   62
The Origins of Art and Ornament   64
The Mesolithic Period   66

Drowned Landscapes   68
The Neolithic Period   70
The Spread of Agriculture   72
Metallurgy   74
The Iron Age   76
Complex Societies   78
Ancient Civilizations   80
Ancient to Recent Past   82
Continental Africa   84
Asia and Australasia   86
The Americas   88
Case Study: Çatalhoyuk   90

Specialisms   **92**
Industrial Archaeology   94
Coastal and Marine Archaeology   96
Churches   98
Buildings   100
Forensic Archaeology   102
A Face from the Past   104
Battlefield Archaeology   106
Ethnoarchaeology   108
Linguistic Archaeology   110
Archaeoastronomy   112
Case Study: Recreating Pugin's House   114

Public Archaeology   **116**
Conservation and Research   118
Getting Involved   120
Learning More   122
Case Study: Jamestown/
   Colonial Williamburg   124

Index   126

Introduction

The popular image of the archaeologist is of an intrepid hole digger looking for buried treasure, probably dressed in eccentric clothes. Though there are some archaeologists that cultivate this image, there are many who work at desks or in laboratories, and that might never have held a trowel in their lives.

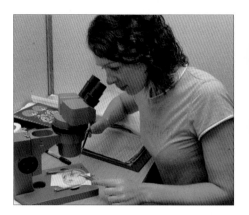

There is far more to the science of archaeology than just searching for and digging up ancient artefacts. Hundreds of different experts are involved in the process, which includes recording, dating and analyzing the finds. This book focuses on the processes and techniques that are involved post excavation.

There are archaeologists in a surprising number of fields: they work in the media, in schools, in parliaments and the civil service, in museums, engineering, publishing and the travel and tourism industries. Some run large public companies or institutions; (for example, the UK's Big Lottery Fund); others are employed by the army, the police and the secret services. Yet others have a day job as a banker or farmer, and turn to archaeology as a weekend hobby. There are even rock star archaeologists (former Rolling Stones guitarist Bill Wyman

has published archaeology books, as has singer Julian Cope, while ex-Beatle Sir Paul McCartney sponsors the UK's annual Conservation Awards).

Archaeologists are not driven by money. While they are not treasure hunters, there isn't an archaeologist alive whose pulse would not quicken at the sight of a beautiful brooch emerging from the soil. However, an archaeologist would not ask 'how much is it worth?', but 'how old is it, why is it here and what can we learn about the maker and the owner?'

Archaeology is rooted in curiosity rather than dreams of wealth, and anybody can become an archaeologist – it isn't necessary to have a university degree or a special licence. If you have ever wondered 'how old is my house, how did the previous inhabitants use the rooms and what did the rooms used to look like?', you are already asking some archaeological questions.

Above Microscopic remains of plants or charred earth are examined as part of the evidence-gathering process.

Riddle solvers

Being interested in the past can be frustrating because the record is so incomplete. Materials tend to survive only if they are durable, such as stone or pottery, or if special conditions prevail, such as permafrost or extreme aridity, (where the air is too dry for the survival of microbes that cause wood, paper, grass, cloth or hair to rot). That is why archaeologists have devised more and more ingenious ways to extract information and meaning from the detritus and accidental survivals of the past. Being unashamed scavengers, archaeologists are also willing to borrow ideas from other disciplines. They have raided the tool chests of historians and linguists, soil scientists and geologists, botanists and anatomists, anthropologists and geographers, and art and architectural historians. More recently, huge strides in archaeological knowledge have been achieved by using scientific and medical technologies – carbon-14 dating, CAT scanning or DNA analysis – as tools for dating the past, looking inside mummified human remains or tracing the genetic origins of people, animals and food plants.

Far Left A student scans sifted soil looking for environmental plant and soil remains.

Left The remains of an ancient irrigation system built by the Nazca people who lived along the southern coast of Peru from 100 to 800 CE.

Above What all archaeologists have in common is that they study the physical remains of the human past, from whole landscapes to microscopic objects, or the symbols left by previous peoples, such as the Sumerian cuneiform script on this tablet recording the distribution of food.

What is archaeology?

There are numerous definitions of archaeology: so many that some people talk about 'archaeologies' in the plural. Some argue that archaeology is a way of thinking, a creative process, others say it is a set of questions about the past, while some define it as the study of human experience – how people have lived in the past and responded to their environment.

There are also many different kinds of archaeologist: some that dig and some that study the results of other people's digs; archaeologists that specialize in a period, a culture, a region or a type of artefact – flint tools or Roman coins, for example. There are landscape archaeologists, terrestrial archaeologists and marine archaeologists (there are no extraterrestrial archaeologists yet, though NASA does employ an archaeologist to study satellite images!).

A winning occupation

All these factors help to answer the question of why archaeology is so fascinating: it is an integrative subject that draws on many other disciplines, it is a subject that touches on all our lives and asks questions about human origins and development, and it leads to a deeper understanding of our world.

This book shows how post-dig archaeology is a process of many stages, from data-gathering, analysing finds, reporting the results, pinning down dates, conducting specialized research and reporting the results.

There is plenty of pleasure and knowledge to be gained from taking part in archaeology, and this book will achieve its aim if it shows you how easy it is to turn from an armchair archaeologist, watching other people doing archaeology on television, into becoming an active archaeologist carrying out your own research.

Below The Roman Forum, with the remains of its ancient government buildings, stands at the centre of the city of Rome.

STUDYING THE FINDS

The excavation is over and the diggers depart with happy memories of a summer spent in the sun, of new friends made and new skills learned, perhaps with a determination to learn more about some aspect of archaeology. However, for the site director, closing the excavation down is not the end of the process at all, but merely the completion of another stage. It has been estimated that about 10 per cent of the effort involved in understanding and researching any one site will go into the desktop assessment phase and another 40 per cent into the excavation, so at this stage the process is now only halfway through. What still lies ahead is the work involved in making sense of the finds. All the information still needs to be linked together into a story that other archaeologists will find useful and that pushes archaeological knowledge forward.

Opposite Carbon-14 tests dated this 'shicra' (woven reed) bag from Lima, Peru, to the 5th century BC.

Above Dendrochronologists date wooden objects by examining the pattern of tree rings and matching them to a dated master sequence.

Above A piece of what is claimed to be Herod's tomb is displayed by archaeologists at a Jerusalem press conference.

Above Coffin furniture, such as these metal spurs retrieved from a grave, may be valuable in dating any bodies found there.

Beginning the Post-Excavation Process

The director now has to make some kind of sense of the catalogue of record sheets, drawings and photographs, not to mention the boxes and bags filled with things found during the excavation. Fortunately, an array of specialists can help analyse the finds and contribute to an understanding of the site.

Above Finds from past excavations in London form a vast study collection for research.

Of course, the director does not simply sit down the day after the dig is over and say 'what does all this mean', because the excavation process itself is an interpretative process. Judgements about what to dig, for example, are based on discussions with diggers and supervisors about the emerging history of the site, its stratigraphy, its phasing and the relationships between features. Finds will have emerged that will have established a broad time period for the use of the site. All of this information is part of the interpretative process.

Because of this process, most directors or project managers will emerge from an excavation with a provisional framework of ideas about the site. The next task is to write about these ideas, while they are still fresh in the mind, and to support the interpretation of the site with evidence from dating, stratigraphy and artefact and ecofact analyses.

Regrettably, there are several reasons why this next stage does not always happen as it should. The director might take a well-deserved vacation, then go back to his or her main job as a university teacher. Some archaeologists write short interim papers and reports featuring the juiciest headline-grabbing findings from the dig, but then lose the will to do the hard work of writing the detailed report. There are also some archaeologists who have never written up the results of major sites that they excavated 30 or more years ago – and the greater the delay the more difficult it is to make a start. It is always easy to put off writing up the site because of 'lack of time or funds'.

The role of the specialist

Perhaps one of the greatest causes of delay in writing up reports is the real shortage of specialists with the knowledge to take material from an excavation, catalogue and analyse it, and produce a report that describes what was found and makes some attempt at saying what it means. Those specialists who are able to do work of this kind are never short of clients; thus the director who approaches a coin or pottery expert for help with the report can expect to have to join a waiting list, and might not know the results for a year or more.

This shortage of specialists is also an opportunity, of course, and it means that any budding pottery, bone, metal-work or coin enthusiast who wants to master the topic will not lack encouragement and help from established specialists. This is a field where there will almost be a guarantee of plenty of future work.

Left Archaeologists at the Arzhan-2 site in the Republic of Tuva, Russia, excavate horse bones from the graves of ancient Scythians, who are known to have revered these animals.

Above Ceramic specialists examine all the finds from an excavation to build up a picture of pottery use at the location.

Presenting the material

The post-excavation process often involves presenting the information learned about the find to other archaeologists and the public. This can include putting some of the material on display in a local museum, giving lectures and writing articles about the site and its finds, presenting the results at academic conferences, perhaps producing a popular publication as well as an academic one, and even taking part in educational initiatives. It will also involve arranging the long-term storage and archiving of all the finds and records so that they are well preserved and are available for other researchers to study.

Above The results of an excavation are presented at an open day.

The post-excavation team

The director will need to call upon the skills and inputs of all types of other people to write up and publish the results of the dig – like many scientific disciplines, archaeology is a highly collaborative process and the director needs to be able to work with, motivate, inspire and manage a wide range of academic, technical and professional specialists. The team that brings all this work to fruition will include photographers and graphics specialists, writers, editors, proofreaders and indexers, layout artists and printers, database experts and web designers, museum curators and education officers, conservators and archivists.

Some of these people have skills that are not specific to archaeology, and increasingly there are opportunities for people who want to pursue a career in archaeology to switch from another skill. For example, people who have trained as editors are in great demand as publications project managers, responsible for resolving any copyright issues that can occur and making sure that all contributors are properly acknowledged. Trained teachers are also in demand because of the educational work carried out by many museums, and graphic artists may contribute to the layout of the reports, or perhaps create finished drawings and reconstructions of what the site might have looked like in the past.

The result of this collaboration will be one or more publications – either printed or accessible on the internet – that tell other archaeologists what has been found. If this is an excavation that is going to continue for several years, the director might publish an interim report, highlighting the year's work and discussing its implications. If the excavation has been completed, the director might publish a definitive report, describing and analysing the site and its significance, with all the supporting evidence.

Right Volunteers and specialists often work together when the excavated find is quite special, as with this cremation burial urn.

Creating a Chronological Framework

A main role of the director or project manager is to explain the development of the site over time. This is often a two-stage process: stage one is to place key changes in the site's history into an order using the site matrix; stage two involves establishing precise dates for the different phases of activity.

Above Careful examination of a potentially dateable timber at the base of a large pit.

In order to tell a coherent story about an excavated site, the director needs to establish a chronological framework – in other words, to be able to say what happened first, what happened next, and so on. Even the simplest of sites has a time dimension: people arrived, cleared the woodland, made fires and inhabited it for a time, then moved on. Many sites have a much more complex history – especially places that have been occupied by people continuously for thousands of years, such as some of the classic sites of the Mediterranean or of the Fertile Crescent region between the Nile, Tigris and Euphrates.

The first key to establishing a chronological framework is the site matrix, which was created during the excavation process by recording every deposit, cut or context. At the end of the excavation, the matrix might consist of numerous jigsaw pieces that have to be fitted together to make a complete picture.

For example, the ditch with the stone culvert that was excavated in the chapter 'Breaking New Ground' forms one piece of the jigsaw. The matrix diagram for that ditch will show a series of numbers (*see* The Site Matrix), each of which represents an event in the process of excavating the ditch, constructing the culvert and refilling the ditch, and corresponds to the strata shown in the section diagram.

However, although the matrix shows the relative sequence of events, three other vital pieces of information are missing: what period of time does each stage in the matrix represent; when did the activity represented by each stage actually take place (what archaeologists call an 'absolute' date); and how do the activities represented by the ditch construction, filling and use relate to all the other events and features that were recorded across the whole of the site? (By confirming this, archaeologists might then ask how the activity on this site fits into the regional, cultural, national or global sequence of events.)

Relative dates

Those are big questions for a site matrix to answer, but that is the challenge. One way the director can fit the jigsaw pieces together is to look for stratigraphic relationships at the points where one feature cuts through another. At the simplest level, anything that is found at the bottom of a ditch will have got into the ditch before anything that is found in the middle, and the contents of the middle layers will have got into the ditch before those of the upper layers. Thus, any

Forming a complete picture of a site

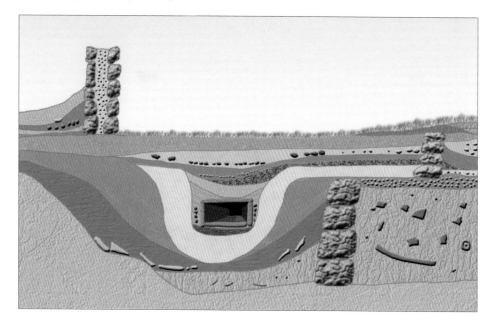

Left By examining other contexts immediately surrounding the stone culvert, archaeologists might conclude that it had been constructed within the natural dip of a silted section of river, to supply a Roman building and jetty (the remains of which are shown buried, right). When the whole area eventually silted up, the site reverted to agricultural land. The ruins of a medieval barn stand above ground, to the left.

Right The remnants of this 13th-century Jewish ritual bath in England forms part of complex foundations relating to London's water supply. Earlier wells, dug during the Roman occupation of the city, were also uncovered during the same rescue excavation, at the site of Blossom's Inn in the east of the city.

layer that lies under another layer must be earlier than that layer and vice versa – the layers at the top are later than those underneath.

At the next level of complexity, one ditch might cross the path of another. Archaeologists will need to know which ditch came first. This can be discovered by using the stratigraphic principles: any feature that is cut by another has to be older and vice versa. The intersection of these two ditches will enable archaeologists to establish a relative sequence: there is now an earlier and later ditch. If either of those ditches intersects with another feature, archaeologists can again establish which came first, so creating relative phasing for three of the sites features – and this process can be used for all the stratigraphic relationships on the site.

Isolated features

In reality, it is rare to pin down the relative chronology of every feature. Most sites have features that exist in isolation – pits, for example – that have no stratigraphic relationship to any other part of the site. Their relationship has to be inferred by other means – if three pits have similar shapes, produce similar pottery and have similar soils, we can hypothesize that they are of similar date, and if one of those pits can be tied stratigraphically to the matrix because it is cut by another feature, all the pits can be given a tentative home in the sequence.

Pinning down key parts of the sequence in relative terms is the first step toward answering the big questions. The next step is to try finding precise dates for parts of the sequence.

Right Examining intersecting contexts in larger, complex sites is a major part of building a complete history of a site.

Using Artefacts as Dating Evidence

There is an unofficial hierarchy in archaeology that places greater emphasis on finds that are capable of yielding dates that can help with the phasing of the site. This often means valuing coins, inscriptions, fine pottery and metalwork above humbler finds.

Above Metal artefacts bearing visible inscriptions, such as this farmer's button, are ideal dating material.

Some types of find – for example, coins, clay tablets, hieroglyphs and inscriptions – incorporate a date as part of their inscription. Or they are inscribed with something that is as good as a date, such as the name of the king or emperor who was on the throne when the object was made. These make it easy to date the piece.

Datable artefacts

For the first 200 years of archaeology, starting in the early 18th century when the discipline first began to form, great effort was invested in building up dated sequences of the most distinctive pottery, jewellery and metalwork forms by looking at the datable objects that they are found with. Initially, this meant focusing on cultures that produced datable material, such as ancient Egypt, Greece, Rome, Byzantium and Arabia.

After establishing chronologies for the materials produced by those civilizations, archaeologists moved out to other cultures, dating their products by looking for deposits that included known and dated products from elsewhere. For example, Egyptian pottery of a known date is often found in association with late Minoan pottery on Crete, enabling the Minoan pottery to be dated on the assumption that it is contemporary with the Egyptian material. Similarly, pottery exported from Europe to the new world during colonial expansion from the 15th century onward can be used to date the indigenous artefacts found with them in archaeological contexts. After many decades of study, archaeologists have worked out dated sequences for many

Above The Roman coin top-left was minted during the reign of Vespasian (who ruled from AD69–79), and recovered from the city of Dorchester in southern England, indicating a very early date for the city's foundation, shortly after the Roman conquest of Britain in AD43. The two other coins date from the third century AD, indicating Dorchester's continuing usage.

Left This Peruvian grave of a warrior-prince contains precious gold finds (the oxidization has turned them green), and associated pottery – both of which may prove datable.

Above Datable finds (*clockwise from top-left*): a broken medieval gaming counter; a Viking brooch; a Roman bone weaving tablet set; and a near-complete dish in Beauvais Sgraffito, luxury French tableware, dated to 16th century.

different styles of pottery, metalwork, jewellery and sculpture. This has enabled them to say with some certainty when an object was manufactured or when it was in fashion.

Residual material

In seeking to pin down dates for the site matrix, the director will start by looking for this type of datable find, while also being wary of making the simplistic assumption that the date of the object provides a date for the context in which it is found. There are all sorts of reasons why this might not be the case, and archaeologists are well aware of the dangers of 'residual' material as well as 'intrusive' material (*see box, right*) misleading them.

By residual, archaeologists mean material that is far older than its context. In February 2007, for example, a metal detectorist unearthed a silver denarius near Fowey in Cornwall, England. Because the coin dated from 146BC – some 189 years before the Romans conquered Britain in AD43 – the find sparked much speculation about whether trade contacts existed between Iron-Age

Britain and Roman Europe at the time. They might well have done, because Iron-Age Cornwall was an important source of metals, such as tin and lead, which were mined at the time. However, the coin simply could not prove, on its own, that such trade took place. The participants in the debate all assumed that the coin arrived in Cornwall around 146BC, whereas it might have been lost hundreds of years later – it might even, for example, have been lost by a modern collector.

Silver and gold objects, jewellery and works of art – all the datable objects that archaeologists like – are the same type of object that people have hoarded for various reasons. They might be passed down the generations as heirlooms, treasured as lucky charms, or simply kept as a safeguard against inflation – silver and gold retain their value better than bronze. Collectors and museum curators from the 19th and 20th centuries are not alone in valuing objects from the past. Many ancient societies placed a value on objects associated with ancestors, and it is common to find old objects placed in coffins and buried with the deceased. Neolithic axes sometimes turn up on Roman sites, and archaeologists sampling the Thames embankment once found the antlers of exotic deer that certainly did not get there on their own.

Above Ripon Cathedral in Yorkshire, England, built using recycled masonry.

Intrusive material

A less common and more easily recognized problem is that of intrusive material, where material from a later date finds its way into earlier contexts. Usually this is the result of some kind of disturbance – for example, animal burrowing is one cause. Wormholes can have a similar effect by creating channels in the soil through which later material drops down through the stratigraphy from the top to the bottom of a ditch. This common phenomenon, where material from one period appears in a connect of a different date, is what motivated astronomers to give the name 'wormholes' to the theoretical corridors in time and space that would allow for the possibility of time travel.

Ancient farming also contributes to the confusion because of the jumble of broken pottery and material from all sorts of dates that accumulates in trash piles and manure heaps that are later taken out and spread on the soil. Some of this material can end up being washed into ditches and pits.

Even what archaeologists call 'robbing' – although in reality the process might be considered 'recycling' – can introduce misleading material into a new context. In medieval Europe, many churches were built from masonry salvaged from ruined Roman buildings.

Earliest and Latest Dates

Two key concepts – terminus post quem (or 'earliest possible date') and terminus ante quem ('latest possible date') – have been developed to enable archaeologists to use artefacts as dating evidence, taking into account the possible longevity of some types of find.

Datable artefacts are treated cautiously, but archaeologists can make statements about them that make logical sense. As a general principle, the different deposits of soil filling a ditch, pit or post hole are likely to be of the same age and date as the artefacts they contain. As long as the fill of the ditch has not been churned up by animal burrowing or ploughing, it would be difficult to think of a scenario to account for interpreting the fill of the ditch as prehistoric if it contained Roman pottery.

Terminus post quem

However, if a datable object, such as a coin, is found within the fill of a ditch, pit or post hole, it is possible to think of various scenarios that might account for its presence in the deposit that should make archaeologists cautious about assuming that it provides a secure date. It is common enough in archaeology to find an object that has been deliberately placed in a ditch, pit or post hole as an offering to the gods and ancestors – such practices continue up to the present day, with 'time capsules' sometimes being included in the foundations of a building.

A Roman coin found at the base of a post hole provides what archaeologists call a *terminus post quem*, meaning that the hole must be later in date than the date at which the coin was struck. In other words, it provides the earliest date in which it is possible for the coin

Above Egyptian mummies entombed in wooden sarcophagi and wearing funerary masks, discovered at the Valley of the Kings, Egypt.

to have got into the post hole. If we know that coins of this type were not struck until AD120, the post hole cannot be earlier than that date, so the building of which the post is part must have been built after AD120.

However, there is another possible scenario that an archaeologist must look out for when using finds as dating evidence. The coin might have got into the fill of the post hole after the building was abandoned. The post itself might have been the central post of a late Iron-Age roundhouse that was constructed in the 1st century BC, but that was, 200 years later, considered old fashioned, smoky and draughty by comparison with the new style of architecture introduced by the Romans. A new stone house was built close by and the old one abandoned, left to collapse or even dismantled, during which time the coin was dropped and rolled into the hole left by the decayed or dismantled post. In this scenario, the coin doesn't date the digging of the post hole, nor the period when it was in use, only the decay of the post. Deciding which of these two scenarios is the correct one will depend on the archaeologists' skill in interpreting the layers that fill the excavated post hole.

Left A poignant image of the remains at Pompeii, near Rome, Italy, where bodies mummified in the ash of a Mount Vesuvius eruption in AD79 are being excavated.

Terminus ante quem

Perhaps of considerably greater value to an archaeologist, although occurring more rarely, is the *terminus ante quem*, which means a date before which an event must have taken place. For example, all the material found beneath the ashes and lava that buried Pompeii in August AD79 must date to before that catastrophic eruption of the volcano of Mount Vesuvius.

Other disasters provide a similar seal on events that enables archaeologists to say that material lower down in the stratigraphic sequence must be older. In London, for example, archaeologists often encounter the deep layer of burning that resulted from the Great Fire of September 1666, while another layer of burning found on many London sites is evidence for the Boudiccan revolt of AD60, when native Britons led by Boudicca attacked and set fire to the Roman city.

Stratified finds

For finds to be of any great value in archaeology as dating evidence, it helps if they come from a sealed context – that is to say, if they come from an undisturbed soil deposit that lies beneath another deposit that is demonstrably ancient – for example, from beneath a Roman mosaic floor. Throughout the excavation, the diggers will have been looking out for exactly this sort of dating evidence. It is not often found, but when it is, it can be the pivot around which the dating and phasing of the site will hinge.

More often, the presence of a datable object in the archaeological record is capable of multiple explanations. Such scenarios should stimulate the archaeologists' powers of imagination and explanation. They are a warning against complacency and the drawing of simplistic conclusions. In response, archaeologists look for patterns of finds across a number of features on the site that are consistent, that reinforce each other, and that seem to tell the same story. They also look for similar patterns on other sites, either in the area or of a similar type elsewhere.

Archaeologists will usually talk about likely scenarios rather than certain ones. In order to see those patterns at all, they need to gather data as objectively as possible, so that other archaeologists can look at the same data subsequently and either agree with their interpretation or argue for a different scenario.

Above The Great Fire of London has left an indelible mark on the archaeological record, in the form of a substantial depth of ash and charred timbers.

The Great Fire

The breadth of charred material buried beneath the modern City of London suggests that, when the owners of destroyed properties built their new homes and shops, they did not bother to tidy away the remains of the old but simply built on top. This is consistent with what we know of the post-Fire history of London. Sir Christopher Wren was asked to create a masterplan for a new city to rise from the ashes of the old, with long straight boulevards and open squares in place of the cramped medieval alleys of pre-Fire London. His plan was never executed because London's merchants, keen to get back to making money, quickly rebuilt their premises using the same property boundaries of old.

Above A Roman mosaic under the foundations of a modern-day hospital is being excavated.

Left The 50-year Belvedere time capsule project, sunk into the ground in 1957, is raised again in Tulsa, Oklahoma.

Radiocarbon Dating

One way to achieve greater certainty in dating is to use radiocarbon dating (also known as carbon-14 dating), which enables organic materials to be dated with an increasing degree of accuracy. Radiocarbon dating literally revolutionized prehistoric archaeology when it emerged in the 1940s.

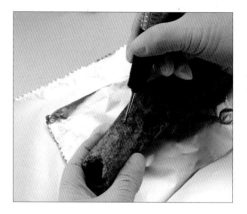

Wartime research into nuclear weaponry led to the development of a peaceful by-product: radiocarbon dating. Until then, prehistoric sites were dated in broad slices of time on the basis of pottery and metalwork typologies, whose accuracy was measured in hundreds or thousands of years. Fragments of a collared urn can tell archaeologists that the site was of a Bronze Age date, but it could not tell precisely when this distinctive type of pottery was made in the Bronze Age – a period spanning 1,500 years or more.

So, for the huge period of time represented by prehistory – literally thousands of years – it was not possible

Below Carbon 14 absorbed by living organisms decays after death (shown top right) at a constant rate; measuring the amount left tells us how long it was since the animal or person died or the plant was cut down.

to do more than make intelligent guesses about the absolute and relative dates of individual sites and their relationships. That inability to say whether one site was earlier or later than another was a major drawback, because one of the key questions in archaeology is how ideas spread – ideas such as agriculture, art, religion, living in cities, kingship, metal-working or fashions in pottery, jewellery or architectural styles – and to provide answers, archaeologists need to have a chronological framework.

The science of radiocarbon dating

That framework fell into place with the discovery that the radioactive isotope of carbon called carbon-14 (which scientists abbreviate to 14C) can be used as a chemical calendar. Carbon-14 is produced by the effects of sunlight

Above Samples from a human femur (thigh) being taken for radiocarbon dating.

on the atmosphere, on the oceans and on plant life. It is in the air we breathe and in the food we eat. All living things absorb it while they are alive – so that animals and plants end up with the same amount of carbon-14 in their cells as there is in the atmosphere.

The moment an organism dies it stops absorbing carbon-14. From that moment on, carbon-14 decays, breaking down chemically and turning into simpler chemicals. Fortunately for archaeologists, carbon-14 decays at a constant and measurable rate. In effect, it provides a clock that starts ticking at

Below Food and drink residues from vessels like this Chinese 'gui' pot, used for making offerings to the gods, can provide organic materials that can be used for carbon dating.

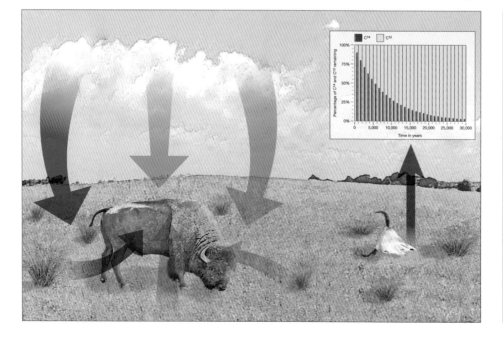

Above A pestle and stone block 'bins', 12th-century corn-grinding equipment found at the Navajo Ancient Monument site in the south-western United States, provide dating material.

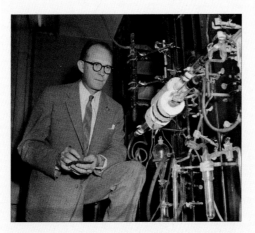

Above Willard Libby stands with the equipment he designed for distilling carbon.

Willard Libby, the father of radiocarbon dating

Willard Frank Libby (1908–80), Professor of Chemistry at the University of Chicago, Illinois, was awarded the Nobel Prize in 1960 for leading the team that cracked the rate at which the radioactive isotope carbon-14 decays. The team developed a technique for measuring carbon-14, which they did by building a sensitive Geiger counter. The team then needed to find some way of calibrating the results they got from measuring the amount of remaining carbon-14 they found in organic materials. They did this by creating tables of carbon-14 in objects of a known date. To go as far back in time as possible, they used timbers from the tombs of ancient Egyptians whose date at death was known from tomb hieroglyphs. Once a sequence of dates was pinned down, it was possible to predict the likely decay rates of carbon-14 for objects up to 50,000 years old.

the moment of death, so in theory archaeologists can determine the date at which a tree was cut down or an animal slaughtered by measuring the amount of radiocarbon in a sample of wood or bone and comparing this to the amount of radiocarbon in the atmosphere (which, at the time when radiocarbon dating was first developed, was assumed to be constant).

The dating revolution

With this discovery, bone, antler and plant material, such as charred wood or grain, took on a new significance in the archaeological record. The immediate effect of radiocarbon dating was to enable archaeologists to revisit classical sites – from Jericho to Stonehenge – seeking material suitable for dating. Early carbon dating was slow, expensive and dependent on a handful of specialists working in nuclear laboratories with priorities other than helping archaeology – such as nuclear power generation and weapons development. Despite this, progress was made and the results overturned many old ideas. Sites were shown to be much older than had been thought and to have been occupied for longer; key developments, such as farming, were shown to have occurred earlier than previously thought, often by thousands of years. Sites that were thought to be younger or older than each other were often proved to be contemporaneous, or vice versa.

A key finding was that farming began in several different parts of the world – as far apart as Africa, Asia and the Americas – at about the same time – opening up all sorts of new questions. Once firm dates could be obtained relatively easily, archaeologists became less obsessed with questions about when things happened and instead began to ask why and how. Did new developments and ideas spread across the globe because people migrated and took new ideas with them? Or did their development of agriculture or metal-

Above Archaeologists remove samples from charcoal pits for radiocarbon dating.

working give them an advantage that enabled them to conquer neighbouring peoples, or to colonize the wilderness more effectively? Did people invent these ideas independently of each other in several places at once? Or do good ideas simply travel very fast, implying that there was a network of contacts and links between different people that effectively spread around the inhabited parts of the world?

Selecting Samples for Carbon Dating

Obtaining radiocarbon dates is no longer a technique that archaeologists employ in only rare and exceptional circumstances. It is now the most commonly used form of scientific dating, so it is vital for archaeologists to know what makes a good sample for the test.

Above These samples are stored in phials to prevent contamination before carbon dating.

From being a very expensive and time-consuming process, radiocarbon dating has now become a routine aspect of archaeological practice, with specialized laboratories providing a fast and relatively inexpensive radiocarbon dating service. Samples for testing are chosen in consultation with a specialist, who will advise on the suitability of the material. A variety of organic materials can be tested, including wood and charcoal, nuts and charred grain, animal and human bone, food remains and shell, cloth, pollen, peat and some soils, and even iron and slag if it contains carbon impurities.

Secure stratification

Experience and judgement are necessary to ensure that the material selected for dating will be able to yield a useful date. The material must come from a securely stratified context – one that excludes intrusive material of a later date. It must have been collected under conditions that will prevent contamination by modern material, which means that it should not be handled or washed.

Residual material – or material that is older than the deposit – must also be excluded. Charcoal twigs or nuts are perfect because they contain carbon-14 that has been absorbed over a very short time period – a year in the case of nuts – and can thus give archaeologists a date that is very close to the date at which the nuts were consumed or the twigs were cut and burned in a fire.

By contrast, wood that comes from the central part of the trunk of a very old tree might give a misleading date because it could have been several centuries old when it was cut down and used – it could then have survived in use – perhaps as part of a building – for several more centuries before being salvaged and used as firewood.

Equally, one must bear in mind that radiocarbon dating gives us a date for the object, and not for its context. For example, a date obtained from pig bones that have been consumed as part of a feast will tell archaeologists the date at which the pig was killed and the meat consumed; it will not necessarily tell the date of the pit, because the bones could have been placed in the pit at a much later date. That is why it is very important to obtain more than one sample from each context. The consistency of the dating from several different samples tells a more convincing story than one date on its own, and this is a problem that has dogged the understanding of the different construction phases at major monuments, such as Stonehenge, where the

Left These remains of a prehistoric cow burial, likely to have been part of a sacrificial ceremony, may provide valuable dates.

Right Helge Stine points at the Newfoundland location containing the remains of a Viking village, which predated Columbus' arrival by some 500 years.

dating rests on isolated samples from antler picks, which might be later than the pits they are found in.

The first American invasion

Sometimes radiocarbon dating can be the conclusive piece of evidence that proves an event that has divided archaeological opinion. The 'Saga of the Greenlanders', for example, is an Icelandic poem that describes the colonization of Greenland by the Norwegian Erik the Red. The saga is preserved in a late 14th century manuscript but describes events that took place around AD970 to 1030. How much of the saga is true and how much is fiction? In particular, did Eric and his followers discover and colonize a part of North America, which they called Vinland (*vin* in Old Icelandic means 'flat' – hence 'flat land', or 'land of plains'), which the saga describes as a land of grassy meadows and salmon-filled rivers?

The evidence needed to authenticate the events described in the saga was found in 1960 when the remains of a Viking village were discovered by the Norwegian explorers and archaeologists, Helge and Anne Stine Ingstad at L'Anse aux Meadows, which is now a National Historical Park on the northernmost tip of the island of Newfoundland, in Canada. Carbon-14 dating of the bone needles and knitting tools was used to date the site to around AD1000.

The saga was shown to be a true account of actual events, and the poem also contained evidence that this early colonial settlement might have been abandoned because of a misunderstanding between the Vikings and the local Algonquin people – the milk served to the Native Canadians by the Vikings at a feast made them sick (probably from lactose intolerance) and so the Vikings were suspected of attempting to poison their guests.

Right Helge Stine points at the Newfoundland location containing the remains of a Viking village, which predated Columbus' arrival by some 500 years.

Turin Shroud

Carbon dating is used to date any objects where precision is required, not just objects from the very distant past. The Catholic Church gave permission in 1988 for a piece of ancient linen from the Turin Shroud to be tested, and that gave a direct date for the shroud of between 1260 and 1390. This accords very well with the first documented account of the Shroud, which dates from 1357, and suggests that the shroud is not that of the historical Jesus. However, scientists remain intrigued by the skill of the medieval makers of the shroud, and have wondered about the exact technique used to create the ghostly image that it preserves.

Below This sample of the Turin Shroud was carbon dated by scientists at Oxford University, England.

Below Though we now know the Turin Shroud is medieval, we still do not know how the haunting image was produced.

Advanced Dating Strategies

Over the last 50 years, carbon-dating techniques have become more and more refined. Accelerator mass spectrometry has developed as a means of dating exceptionally old deposits, and statistical methods have been developed for achieving greater accuracy.

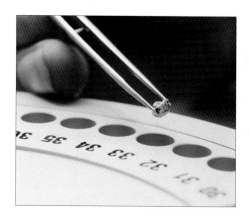

Above A sample about to be incinerated via AMS to measure the degree of carbon decay.

Although most organic materials can be tested for their carbon-14 content, a considerable weight of material might be necessary to yield meaningful results using conventional carbon-dating techniques. Dating laboratories specify a minimum weight of 1g (⅒oz) of wood or charcoal, 5g (⅕oz) of peat or 50g (1¾oz) of bone – but ideally they prefer much more than this: 12g (⅖oz) of wood, 10g (⅓oz) of charcoal and 100g (3½oz) of bone are the ideal. What is more, dating specialists prefer to have two separate samples whenever possible to act as a control. If both samples yield a similar date, you can have some confidence that the samples are uncontaminated by residual or intrusive material.

Splitting atoms

However, what if you only have a tiny amount of material. For example, a single carbonized grain of wheat from a hearth that you think might represent the last human activity before the abandonment of a site. The answer is to use the more expensive and sophisticated accelerator mass spectrometry (AMS) technique, which can yield results from as little as 10mg of material – equivalent to the weight of one cereal grain, or the residues of food contained in the porous vessel walls of a pot.

In basic terms, this works by bursting the atoms apart that make up the sample, and measuring the different amounts of each element. To do this requires equipment that is expensive to build and run, but it is a much more sensitive technique for measuring carbon-14 and can extend the time period for dating ancient material back to 70,000 years ago.

Beyond this date the amount of residual carbon-14 in any sample is so low that it cannot be distinguished from the natural background radiation that exists all around us. Even so, AMS is an important technique for dating early hominid migrations and activities – for example, the spread of our ancestors, Homo sapiens, into Asia and Australia – and for dating the last populations of Neanderthals to survive in Europe, before their final extinction, which is currently dated to around 24,000BC.

New dates for old

Every so often, carbon dating undergoes a mini-revolution when new tests are carried out on material that has already been dated using methods that have been superseded. Much of the redating activity of the last decade has been necessary to eliminate errors in the formulae previously used to turn radio-carbon data into calendar dates. Scientists now know, for example, that the rate of decay of carbon-14 is slower than the figures used by Libby's team when they first developed carbon-dating in the 1940s. The half life of

Left A scientist using computerized equipment to control an AMS experiment.

carbon-14 (the time it takes for the amount of the radioactive isotope carbon-14 to decay) is 5,730 years rather than 5,568 years.

Scientists also know that the amount of carbon-14 in the atmosphere is not constant, but fluctuates, sometimes as the result of sunspot activity and sometimes for reasons that can be observed but that are not understood. Scientists have discovered, too, that not all organisms absorb carbon-14 at the same rate, and that some organisms (especially fish and shellfish) are capable of continuing to absorb carbon in sea water even after death.

Dates derived from measuring carbon-14 have been calibrated with dates from other scientific techniques to investigate and iron out these discrepancies. Armed with all this mass of new data, archaeological scientists have been able to reduce the level of error, at the same time increasing the level of certainty that the dates they provide are accurate.

The meaning of carbon-14 dates in archaeology

Dates are usually expressed in archaeological reports according to a standard format. In general, the report will give the name of the laboratory that under-took the tests, the unique sample number, an archaeological reference number that ties the sample to the site and context from which it was excavated, and then a date.

The date itself is written in a form that expresses the likelihood of the date falling within a certain range. For example, the date 1770–1630BC given in the laboratory report means that there is a 95 per cent certainty that the date falls within the range 1770 to 1630BC. An alternative might be to give the date as 1700±70 (give or take 70 years), which means there is a 95 per cent chance that it lies in the range 1770 to 1630BC. The 140 date range is there because radiocarbon dating is not a pinpoint accurate science. Alternatively, those same dates might be expressed as 3650±70 BP, where BP stands for 'before present' –

Dating America's Clovis culture

Archaeologists believe that the first migrants to arrive in the Americas belonged to the Clovis culture – hunter-gatherers with distinctively shaped spear points first found in Clovis, New Mexico. However, when did they arrive? Clovis artefacts were first dated in the 1960s and 1970s, using carbon-dating techniques that are now obsolete, and gave a date of 13,600 years ago. However, those same artefacts were redated in 2006 using AMS. The results show that Clovis technology is younger than previously thought – 13,100 years old – and lasted only 200 to 350 years. The result introduces all kinds of new questions: is 350 years long enough for those people to have spread from the Siberian land bridge all the way to the tip of South America? Some say 'yes', while others argue it would take 1,000 years. If so, this raises the intriguing possibility that there were people already in the Amercias before the Clovis people arrived, and that the rapid dissemination of Clovis spear points is explained by these earlier people adopting Clovis technology.

Left Clovis spear points, made of fine-grained stone called 'chert'.

however, 'present' doesn't mean today but rather 1950, the date at which this dating convention was established.

Bayesian statistics

A recent development – so recent that its implications are still being assessed – is the use of Bayesian statistical techniques, designed to reduce the errors in probability calculations. Named after the 18th-century mathematician Thomas Bayes, the theory behind Bayesian statistical techniques is far from new. However, the application of these methods has had to wait for the availability of computers with sufficient speed and power to do the vast amounts of repetitive calculations, or number crunching, involved.

The benefit is that it is becoming possible to give precise calendar dates to radiocarbon samples, rather than date ranges, and some surprising results have already been achieved. For example, Neolithic long barrows in Europe are now thought to have been fashionable for a very short period of time – perhaps no more than 100 years – rather than, as was previously thought, having been a burial practice in use for more than 1,000 years.

Above Carbon dating tells us that 'Wayland's Smithy' chamber tomb, in Oxfordshire, England, was built around 3700BC.

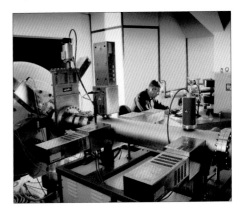

Above Scientists can get dates from a single cereal grain using sophisticated equipment like the mass spectrometer.

Dendrochronology and Other Dating Methods

Trees are especially responsive to environmental fluctuations, and differences in temperature, sunlight and rainfall from one year to the next are reflected in their annual growth rings. As a result, tree-ring dating has become the second most important dating method commonly used in archaeology.

Above Wet or dry summers create unique and dateable patterns of wide and narrow tree rings.

The knowledge that trees have annual growth rings existed as far back as the 15th century, which is when the first historical records speak of counting rings to gauge the age of a tree. However, the use of these rings as a means of giving precise dates to buildings and archaeological sites did not develop until the 1920s. This practice is known as dendrochronology.

One of the pioneers of the technique was A.E. (Andrew Ellicott) Douglass (1867–1962), an American astronomer who looked for evidence of the way that plants might respond to sunspot activity and found a correlation between tree-ring width and solar variation. He did this by looking at the tree rings in timbers from ancient Native American villages in Arizona and New Mexico, and comparing them with sunspot activity records dating back to the 17th century. These records were found in journals kept by scientists such as William Herschel.

Tree-ring research

Douglass subsequently established the Laboratory of Tree-Ring Research at the University of Arizona. He then compared tree-ring evidence from 4,000 year old bristle-cone pine tree trunks preserved in the White Mountains of California with climate records from ice cores, glaciers, lake and seabed deposits and volcanic events. As the research became international in scale, ancient wood from all kinds of sources was added into the study, with samples coming from bog oak – ancient tree trunks preserved in peat bogs in northern Europe – and timbers from ancient buildings, such as the great cathedrals built in Europe.

Little by little a sequence of annual rings was built up that now covers the period back to 10,000BC. There are gaps in the record, and there are many regional variations, due to localized forest fires, volcanic eruptions or periods of severe cold, that are not fully charted. However, despite these problems, master sequences have been built up for whole regions of the world for trees growing in the same geographical zone and under similar climatic conditions. Thus, it is now possible to date ancient timbers with a high degree of precision by taking a sample and matching the pattern of narrow and thick rings from the sample to the regional sequence.

Understanding the results

As always with archaeological dating, the result cannot always be taken at face value. Exact dates for the felling of a tree can be given only if the bark survives or one of the five outer rings just below the bark. This is the part of a tree that is often trimmed off before the timber is used for building purposes. Where it has been removed, or where the timber comes from the central part of the tree, it is better to

Left Tree rings have been used to date the construction of London's medieval waterfront to the early 13th century.

Above Slivers of wood examined by microscope reveal their unique ring pattern.

date the timber by using radiocarbon dating, because that will provide a more accurate date for the felling. Fortunately, bark does often survive in structures that are not intended to be seen – hidden in roofs or buried below ground. Waterlogged timbers from Roman bridges and forts in Germany and the Netherlands have been dated precisely, as have timbers from medieval and Roman waterfronts in London and several Russian and Scandinavian cities. In London, for example, dendro dating has changed the accepted date of the founding of Roman London's timber quays to before the Boudiccan revolt of AD60, rather than after.

Other dating techniques

Archaeologists of today are in a privileged position, because scientists have developed a battery of techniques for dating glass, volcanic ash, obsidian, burnt flint and stone, tooth enamel, pottery and burnt clay, wood, shell, plants and seeds – to name just some of the possibilities. There is a repertoire of dating techniques that, in theory, can be used to obtain absolute dates for any of the sites being excavated. Archaeologists need to know what works best given the age of the site and the type of material available for testing. Tree-ring dating provides the most accurate results for relatively recent sites, while carbon dating is best for older sites, and others – such as potassium-argon dating – are better for very old sites.

Above Archaeologists look for timbers with some bark left on them because the outer five layers tell you exactly when the tree was felled.

A number of specialized dating techniques are based on heating samples of material, then detecting the presence of different elements and their isotopes in the resulting gases. This is the basis of potassium-argon and argon-argon dating, which are used for dating ash, lava and volcanic materials, and also for fossilized bones found in volcanic rocks. For example, potassium-argon dating was used to date Lucy – the famous hominid found in Ethiopia – and the early hominids found in Tanzania's Olduvai Gorge.

Another method used for dating objects is optical, or luminescence, dating. This technique looks for electrons that are trapped or fixed into minerals at the very precise moment that they are exposed to intense light or heat – for example, when clay is fired to create pottery. These can be released and measured either by heating them again, known as thermoluminescence (TL) dating, or by stimulating specific electrons using blue, green or infrared light, which is called optically stimulated luminescence (OSL) dating or photoluminescence (PL) dating.

Above Sand from this hearth in Mungo National Park, Australia, was used for dating the ancient settlement site.

Grains of truth

PL dating has been used effectively to date layers of sand in Australia that cover deposits containing human artefacts. It has shown that people were present at the site up to 60,000 years ago. TL dating has also been used to detect ceramic pieces fraudulently claimed to be ancient. These forgeries lack the trapped electrons that should be there if the ceramic piece had genuinely been fired in antiquity.

Finds and Typologies

Long before the scientific techniques were developed for dating organic materials by physical and chemical means, archaeologists adopted the idea of taxonomy – the classification of objects on the basis of their similarities and differences – from botany and the natural sciences.

Taxonomy remains a key technique in archaeology for establishing what the finds from a site can tell us. Once the director or project manager has made decisions about which samples from the site should be packed up and sent to the dating laboratory, the next task is to tackle the rest of the finds from the site. It is unlikely that a director will have the detailed knowledge to analyse the finds without help, so an army of finds specialists will be recruited.

Some archaeologists have built their career not on digging but on getting to know a particular type of find, such as pottery, metalwork, bone, snail and shell, pollens or plant material. Others specialize in ancient building materials,

worked stone, woodwork, coins, leather or textiles, jewellery and personal adornments, glass, statuary or painted wall plaster. Within these broad categories, there might be sub-specialities: some pottery experts only study fine tablewares, amphorae (storage jars), clay lamps, glazed pottery or grass-tempered wares. The skills they possess might have been established by studying a particular class of find for a university research thesis, and then working with that material as a museum curator. They can be depended on to identify accurately the material they are sent, a skill that takes years to develop, through constant handling of the material.

Above Some of the finds from the Royal Arsenal site at Woolwich, UK, include these shot cases as well as lead shot and pottery.

The critical task for the director is to harness the expertise of the best people available. The specialist will normally charge a fee for the work based on an assessment of how many days of work are involved and the complexity of the task.

Typologies

Once the boxes of finds land on the desk of the finds specialist, there are all kinds of questions to be asked. The first and most essential task is to describe what has been found, and to compare

Left and above Specific sites yield very particular categories of find. The 'common finds' pictured above (from the industrial site, *shown left*) are well documented. Existing typologies categorizing styles of metals, leather goods, earthenware, pottery and glassware enable archaeologists to identify and date similar artefacts recovered on site very quickly.

the material from the particular site with what has been found on similar sites elsewhere.

It is rare that a site will yield any finds that are truly new and unique, although this can happen, especially when dealing with sites whose special environment (cold, dry or water-logged) preserves organic remains. More typically, every single find from the site can be placed within an existing framework, or 'typology'. Borrowing principles of classification from the biological sciences, archaeologists have been building up these typologies for the last 150 years, classifying the most common finds from excavations according to their characteristics and their stratigraphic relationships.

Changes over time

Stratigraphy is one of the key principles of archaeological classification because it prevents archaeologists from making simplistic judgements about the material and sorting it according to subjective ideas, such as the commonly held belief that objects become more complex over time. Faced with a pile of unstratified pottery, it would be tempting to sort them on the assumption that the crudest and simplest shapes might be the earliest, and that as potters became more skilled at their craft, the pottery would become more sophisticated, better made, more elaborate and more diverse in form. This was indeed the sort of assumption that was made by early antiquaries in the 17th and 18th centuries.

However, careful scientific recording of what is found in each layer or context on the site can lead to a different conclusion. Putting the pottery in stratigraphic order, from the earliest layers to the latest, will show how shapes, decoration and materials really change over time. This will reveal the true pattern of development, which is often more interesting than simplistic 'evolutionary' notions based on aesthetic judgements about what looks most sophisticated to the modern eye. Using this scientific

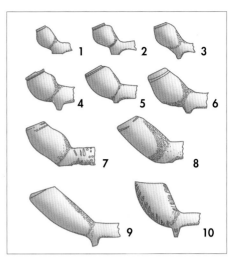

Above This typology of clay pipes spans some 260 years; note how the style of the 'bowls' becomes larger as tobacco becomes cheaper. Dates are as follows: **1:** 1580–1610; **2–5:** 1610–40; **6–7:** 1640–60; **8:** 1660–1710; **9:** 1690–1710; **10:** 1820–40.

approach, archaeologists have been able to build typologies for most of the common types of find – and in some cases have been able to give precise dates to those sequences.

Rediscovering Roman Germany

The classification of armour, brooches and fine tableware from early Roman military sites in Germany has had a significant impact on archaeologists' understanding of Roman artefacts. The campaigns that the Romans fought in their attempts to conquer Germany between the late 1st and late 2nd centuries were recorded by historians, such as Tacitus, and are represented by the remains of forts and frontiers established season by season, according to the fortunes of the army as they advanced or retreated along the banks of the Rivers Rhine and Danube.

This unique combination of historical and archaeological evidence has enabled German scholars, many of them working at the Deutsches Archäologisches Institut founded in 1902, to build the typologies that are still being used by archaeologists studying the Roman Empire for dating commonly found Roman objects, such as Samian pottery, military weapons, belt fittings and the shoulder brooches used to pin cloaks and tunics.

Left Finds recovered at the site of the Roman imperial baths of Kaiserthermen in German's Rhineland suggested continued usage from the Neolithic to the Classical period.

Building Typologies

The task of creating typologies is one of the great ongoing tasks of archaeology; and archaeologists who specialize in finds are always on the lookout for opportunities to make their name by contributing new forms, new dates or revisions to existing typologies.

Much of the work that a specialist does is routine and repetitive, and involves classifying and describing finds that are mostly familiar and commonplace. However, the work also has some challenges, because the placing of objects within a typographical scheme involves familiarity with scores of often-obscure reports and articles in archaeological journals. Although typologies are critical to archaeological analysis, a specialist cannot simply buy a book called 'Everything you might want to know about Bronze-Age axe heads'. Instead, the typology for axe heads is widely dispersed in articles and papers that have been published over the last 100 years, and part of the training that the (often self-educated) specialist undergoes is to master the scores of reports in which bits of the typology are described.

Every so often someone might bring the current state of knowledge together in a 'corpus' – a definitive statement of all that is currently known about a class of object. Yet that corpus will be out of date before it is printed, because archaeological knowledge is constantly being refined by new discoveries – and that is what motivates the specialists to do the routine work. Every excavation has the potential to refine the sequence, fill in missing gaps, to provide firm dates for parts of the sequence or even to start an entirely new typology, classifying a neglected or little-studied type of find.

Above Beads were recovered during an excavation in Sinai, Egypt. Samples of lava taken from the same site have been linked to a catastrophic eruption on Santorini in 1500BC, which wreaked havoc along the Egyptian coast.

Contributing to new knowledge

People who are steeped in knowledge about their particular field are always looking for material that could lead to a new research project or help them make their mark by publishing a new class of objects. For example, archaeologists specializing in metalwork have in recent years begun to realize that some of the finds that they have described as having an unknown function might have been made to decorate furniture, such as chairs, chests and couches. This realization has led to a new search through the archaeological record for similar material, along with the creation of new typographies.

Finds made by metal detectorists have also sparked new lines of specialist study into medieval shoe buckles, cap badges, belt fittings and ornate metal dress hooks. The latter is a type of fastening that preceded buttons and is known about from 16th-century portraits of well-dressed ladies and gentleman; however, they have only recently been recovered from archaeological contexts.

Left Hunter-gatherer artefacts are tagged in Spila Cave, Croatia. Finds associated with this location have contributed to knowledge about the ancient Illyrian people, who inhabited the Adriatic site during the Hellenic period.

Right This Romano–British brooch, cleverly cast from a single piece of bronze, reflects the style known as the 'Colchester-type' jewellery.

The refinement of typographies is the basis of much of the research that occurs in universities. The excavation director, when looking for specialists to describe and interpret the finds, will often turn to research graduates for help. The director knows that these researchers can, in turn, call on their supervisors and other experienced professionals for assistance if necessary.

Assemblages

Whereas the specialist is concerned with one type of material and its typologies, the person who writes the overall site report has to think in terms of the totality of the evidence – what archaeologists call the 'assemblage'. Assemblage simply means a collection of objects found in association with one another. The word is used to describe not just the contents of one pit, but also the contents of the entire site, and it can also be used to describe bigger collections of related materials. Archaeologists will sometimes talk about regional assemblages of material that reflect cultural differences, or period assemblages – meaning the typical mix of finds that tells archaeologists that the site is from the Neolithic Age rather than the Bronze Age.

Like the specialist, the director will be seeking to compare the assemblage from this particular site with others that are similar. Whether a specialist or project manager, the focus will be continually shifting back and forth between the one site and the larger picture of all similar sites, in order to try to pin down as clearly as possible the sequence of activity at the particular site. During the process, stratigraphy will be used to work out relative dates and scientific dating techniques will give precise dates to parts of the sequence wherever possible, filling out the picture by drawing on dating evidence from other sites that are similar in terms of their individual finds or their assemblages.

Above This assemblage of flint tools, all from the same excavation site, includes material that dates from the Mesolithic, Neolithic and Bronze Ages.

Archaeology is a combination of collaborative work and solo study, and perhaps the loneliest task of all is that faced by the director when it comes to combining the evidence from all of the specialist reports and understanding what they mean for the site as a whole.

Above A reconstruction of a typical Anglo-Saxon settlement based on information from assemblages.

Assemblages and diet

When archaeologists study assemblages, it is not the presence or absence of a type of material that is diagnostic so much as the relative proportions. For example, a list of animal bones from a pit will provide an archaeologist with some idea of the main sources of animal protein in the diet, but the proportions of pig to sheep to cow will tell more about the respective contribution that each makes to the diet – perhaps showing that sheep is the main meat consumed and that pig is rare. The assemblage can be further defined in terms of the types of bone from each animal. If whole animals are consumed, perhaps this is a subsistence household, eating all they produce, whereas selective cuts might suggest a household that can select its meat and perhaps buys from a butcher rather than rearing their own animals. Another refinement might be to look at the age of the animals at slaughter, which can indicate a preference for young animals, such as suckling pig or goat, or that most of the meat is consumed in the winter, perhaps as part of a ritual.

Assemblages also yield important information when compared to other assemblages of a similar date. In one example, the study of food remains has been used to identify pockets of people of different ethnicity on the basis of the presence or absence of specific herbs and seasonings. In another example, regional differences in diet have been detected from the difference in cooking pots, with one region favouring slow-cooked casseroles and another preferring grilled foods.

Seriation and Trends

What happens if an archaeologist is working on an excavation site that consists of separate features, that do not appear to have any stratigraphic relationships, and no material has been found that can be used for absolute dating? The answer is to deploy mathematics.

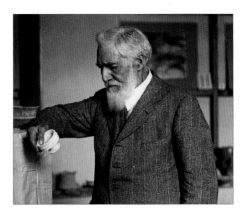

Above Sir Flinders Petrie (1853–1942) with pottery he recovered from southern Palestine.

Classical sites in Europe are rich in the kinds of finds that can be dated by stratigraphic relationships, scientific dating, typography or assemblage. However, this isn't a luxury that every archaeologist can count on. In the United States and Australia, for example, the evidence from a site can consist entirely of a scattering of finds from the surface of the soil – with no stratigraphy and no intersecting features to provide clues about the phasing or dating of the site.

Faced with such situations, archaeologists have developed the techniques of seriation based on multi-variate analysis. As the latter term suggests, this involves looking at the many variable characteristics that distinguish one assemblage of finds from another – instead of placing one type of find into a typology – for example, a bronze brooch, a coin, or a piece of decorated

Samian ware – seriation tries to place the whole assemblage into a typographical sequence.

Fickle fashion

This idea was pioneered by Sir William Flinders Petrie (1853–1942), one of the founders of modern archaeological method. Digging a cemetery at Diospolis Parva in Upper Egypt in 1928, he devised a new system for analysing the contents of the graves that contained nothing that could be dated using the methods of his day and that could not be dated relatively through their stratigraphy because none of the graves touched or cut any of the others.

Instead, Flinders Petrie decided to look at the percentage of each type of artefact in each grave, and then to look for patterns. He represented each grave on a piece of paper and shuffled the papers until he had a sequence that

made sense to him, based on the underlying assumption that pottery styles come in and out of fashion, one style being pushed out by another. Instead of assuming that a style could be in fashion for a long time, and that many styles can co-exist, he assumed that fashions were fickle and short lived, and looked for patterns based on the shortest period of time between the appearance of a style and its replacement by another.

To give a simplified example, if grave 1 contains 10 per cent of pottery style A and 90 per cent of pottery style B, grave 2 contains 90 per cent of pottery style A and 10 per cent of pottery style B, and grave 3 contains 50 per cent of each, Flinders Petrie reasoned that grave 3 overlapped into the two other periods, and the correct date sequence was either 1–3–2 (pottery style A is in the ascendancy) or 2–3–1 (pottery style B is growing in popularity). Adding data from further graves might indicate which is the case, as would analysing not just two pottery variables, but several distinctive artefact

Left Based on the clay pipes typology (*see page 143*), this imaginary scenario reflects how assemblages of pipes recovered from three riverside locations can be used to date those sites. Here, the excavation beneath the bridge revealed the greatest percentage of the earlier styles of pipe, so this is probably the oldest location. The pub ruins are perhaps the newest location, with the greatest percentage of pipes reflecting later styles.

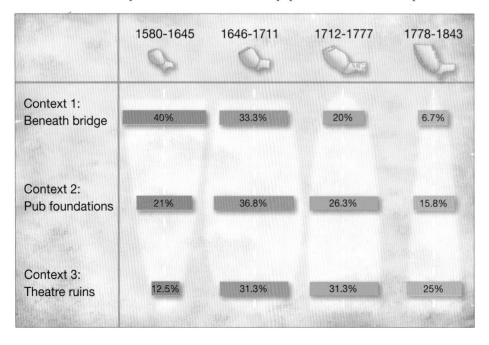

	1580-1645	1646-1711	1712-1777	1778-1843
Context 1: Beneath bridge	40%	33.3%	20%	6.7%
Context 2: Pub foundations	21%	36.8%	26.3%	15.8%
Context 3: Theatre ruins	12.5%	31.3%	31.3%	25%

types and characteristics — flint blades as well as pottery, for example, and decorative motifs and vessel shape.

Computer analysis

What Sir Flinders Petrie did in his head with slips of paper is now done by computer, swapping the mind-bending effort of detecting patterns in multi-dimensional data for computer programs that can define and compare assemblages swiftly, accurately and comprehensively. There is also now the benefit of carbon dating, so that some assemblages can be given an absolute date because of their association with a camp fire, hearth or kiln.

Many such analyses have proven that Sir Flinders Petrie was essentially correct in his assumptions about fashion. The typical result of seriation analysis is the so-called battleship curve — the graphic representation of the frequency with which an object, such as an arrowhead or a pottery shard with a particular type of decoration occurs over time as a percentage of various assemblages. The curve is narrow when the object first appears, widens as it grows in popularity and then tapers off again to a point as it slowly declines in frequency.

The transition from one style to another is not abrupt — different types overlap as one slowly replaces another. One archaeologist has likened this to what you see every day on the streets. Count the number of cars that are one, two, three and four years old and work out the percentage that each makes of the total. The result is likely to be a similar battleship curve, with very few brand new models, a growing proportion of cars that are two, three, and four years old, perhaps reaching the bulge of the curve at between four and five-year-old models, followed by a declining number of six, seven, eight and nine year old models and very few cars over ten years old.

Right An archaeologist examines pottery goods from the oldest-known Mayan royal tomb, found in Guatemala. The tomb dates from 150BC.

Above Pottery from Port St Charles, Barbados, both dating from AD600–800. (*Top*) cream slip with red and black slip decoration; (*bottom*) cream slip with red and white slip decoration.

Pottery from prehistoric Barbados

Trying to set up a sequence of pottery for prehistoric Barbados, archaeologists looked for various indicators that might have chronological significance. Decoration was one clue, but that was confined to a very small number of shards, so other characteristics were studied, leading to the conclusion that the thickness of the pottery was a vital clue, along with the shape and thickness of the rim of the vessel. The thicker the shards the later they were likely to be, and the finer the earlier (perhaps the reverse of what a crude evolutionary belief might suggest, which is that pottery gets finer as time advances).

The archaeologists then looked at the slip – a type of coloured liquid clay – used to coat the pottery, in combination with decoration. They sorted shards into combinations of finger-marking with cream slip, finger-marking with red slip and finger-marking with polychrome (more than one colour) slip. Comparison with similar pottery from neighbouring islands has suggested that this is a sequence that holds true for a substantial part of the Caribbean and the next stage of research is to try and detect what influence the styles of one island might have on the styles of another.

Ancient Environments

So far, the value of finds has been described largely in terms of what they can tell archaeologists about the date of the site from which they were recovered. However, objects contain many different levels of meaning that go well beyond their value as dating evidence.

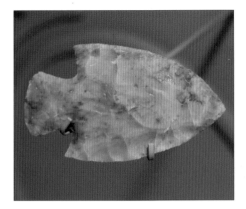

Using finds to provide dates – or date ranges – enables the director to phase the various activities and events that went on at the site. He or she can look at the site's history, from its first use through various changes and peaks and troughs in activity, can look for any gaps in occupation and use, and can look for evidence of continuity of use or eventual abandonment. However, looking for chronological evidence of this kind cannot be divorced from answering a set of questions about what exactly was the nature of the activity that went on at the site and what was the relationship between the people who used the site and their environment, and between the site and its wider landscape setting.

Starting with the environment

Some archaeologists believe that the environment can be a critical factor in determining how people live. For example, a stressful environment can encourage innovative responses and evolutionary change, or it can make life so difficult that populations plummet and people migrate in search of better conditions. Conversely, a benign climate might lead to the plentiful food resources that foster wealth creation, hierarchies, patronage and art, fashion and innovation.

Proving any of these hypotheses will require data about the climate and vegetation. Extracting such information is the task of the environmental

Above Prehistoric hunting tools were recovered from the Arctic tundra on the coast of Alaska in the United States.

archaeologist, whose post-excavation activity will consist of examining and identifying the organic materials recovered from the site. These include the snails, seeds and pollens and any diagnostic elements in the soil that can indicate fires, human occupation or animal husbandry.

Analysing pollen

Pollen samples from a site can be used to create a pollen profile. However, because pollen is so light and can be carried considerable distances by the breeze, archaeologists cannot always

Right Inca storehouses in Peru held emergency supplies of clothing, weaponry and food for times of war or famine.

Above The task for the environmental archaeologist is to present a picture of life at the location by analysing pollen profiles and geological evidence.

be very precise about the specific character of a small plot of land, but it can show what plants were growing in the vicinity of the site and in what quantities. This can serve as a powerful corrective to any ideas about the site that might be derived from its current environment. Many prehistoric burial mounds and henge monuments, for example, are now highly visible structures that can be viewed from afar across fields or pasture – but was this always the case? How would it effect our interpretation if archaeologists discovered that Stonehenge was originally built not on a chalk plain but in a clearing in the dense forest?

Pollen analysis will show whether or not the area was wooded, and whether the woodland species were typical of the so-called 'wildwood', the indigenous natural vegetation of the region, or whether the species were typically of forest clearance and the selection of trees for food (hazel) or basket making (willow), or fencing and building materials (elm, hazel or oak).

Because weeds and wildflowers are specific to certain habitats – woodland, woodland margin, open pasture, cultivated soils, wet, dry, sunny or shady – the weed seed assemblage contributes to the picture of the environment. Snails are habitat specific, too, so their presence is another element that can be considered.

The bigger picture

Broadening out from the immediate environment of the site itself, an environmental archaeologist will try to set the local environmental data into the wider context of what is known about the climatic and vegetational conditions at the time. The picture of ancient weather patterns has been derived from studying ice cores – taken from glaciers or ice caps that have taken centuries to build up, with a new layer of snow being added every year, capturing data about the weather and vegetational conditions that year. Similar data can be obtained from lake and sea-bed sediments, tree-ring data, and volcanic debris. All of this data can be

Above A collection of Minoan pottery was recovered from the island of Crete.

Minoan Crete

The most controversial example of changes within a society due to environmental changes is the rapid collapse of the Minoan civilization on Crete. This has been blamed on the eruption of Thera – a volcanic island 100km (62 miles) from Crete – causing tsunamis, blotting out the sun and choking off plant life. There is no doubt that the eruption would have caused a significant climate upset for the eastern Mediterranean region, but the theory has been challenged because of the gap of a century or more in the date of the eruption and the date for the collapse of the major palace cultures of Minoan Crete.

An alternative theory is that Minoan palace culture ended in a series of co-ordinated palace coups, in which formerly obedient subjects turned on their priest rulers because they were no longer able to guarantee plentiful harvests (and there is evidence for this in the number of palaces that seem to have been deliberately set on fire). Another theory says that the main effect of the eruption was to disrupt trade so that grain could no longer be imported to the island of Crete from other parts of the eastern Mediterranean to feed the population, resulting in mass starvation. Whatever is the explanation, we know that child sacrifice was practised in the final days of the Minoan palace culture, suggesting a degree of desperation and a desire to placate the angry gods.

used to detect climatic differences, especially the very large and cataclysmic events, such as volcanic eruptions, whose effects on weather and crops has often been linked directly to archaeological events and the collapse of whole civilizations.

Climate change is also one of the favoured theories for the evolution of our ancestors, the bipedal apes. They left the protection of jungle canopy, where they used their arms and knuckles for movement, and adapted to the savannah, where they walked on two feet, because the rainforest began to contract.

Further environmental stress might lie behind the migration of humans out of their eastern African homeland. Because arid desert conditions spread, populations began to compete for food and water, travelling further to hunt or gather food.

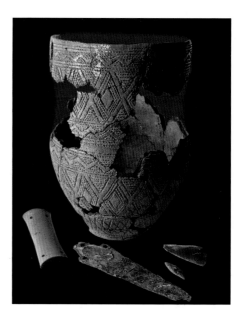

Above Exceptionally well-preserved early Bronze-Age beaker, wristguard, flint knife, awl and bronze dagger from a burial site at Ferry Fryston in Yorkshire, England. These were excavated during motorway construction work.

The Human Response to Climate Change

As well as reconstructing the immediate environment around the site, archaeologists can understand how the site evolved during a period of time by looking for clues about the way that humans responded to their environment and modified what they found.

Above Today's remote and hostile environments may once have been more accessible.

It can be easily argued that one of the defining characteristics of human beings is that we modify our environment to a far greater degree than any other life form. It is true that birds build nests, beavers cut down trees and make lodges and dams, and other primates use tools. However, *Homo sapiens* has responded to the environment in far more complex ways, in terms of the variety and scale of our buildings, settlements, agricultural practices and industries, religious rites and burial practices. It is the job of the site director writing the results of an excavation to try to explain clearly what the specific site represents in terms of human activity and the ways that humans modified the landscape and environment that they inhabited.

Camp fires

Sometimes that modification is simple: some sites consist of only a patch of burnt earth. In fact, the earliest evidence of humans in the landscape often comes from nothing more tangible than an area of burnt earth, said to represent hearths or camp fires. Part of the evidence for early migration into the Americas comes from such hearths, some of which have been dated to 15,000BC or even earlier.

This dating contradicts the widely accepted date of roughly 13,000 years ago for the first migrants crossing into North America via the land bridge linking Siberia and Alaska. The land bridge was created by ice-age conditions, where sea levels fell because atmospheric moisture fell as snow, creating the ice sheets and glaciers that reindeer crossed in search of food, followed by Asian hunters. For humans to have arrived before the land bridge existed implies the ability to cross large expanses of ocean, so debate rages about whether these areas of burning really are the result of human activity or of lightening strikes and forest fires.

Stone scatters

More demonstrably human in origin are the scatters of debris from tool-making – often in association with food remains, such as bone. These represent some of the earliest material evidence for the presence of humans. The Qinghai-Tibetan Plateau is one of the most inhospitable places on the earth, yet archaeologists surveying the shores of the Qinghai Lake, at an elevation of

Left Despite its seemingly barren and impenetrable landscape, the Qinghai-Tibetan mountain range in China was once home to many prehistoric lakeland communities.

3,200m (10,500ft), have found hearths dating from 13,000 years ago along with burnt cobbles used for boiling and degreasing, debris from toolmaking and the bones of a gazelle-sized animals.

Archaeologists excavating in Edmonton, Canada, have also found evidence of butchery, this time from about 10,000 years ago, in what has been dubbed the Quarry of the Ancestors. It is located approximately 75km (50 miles) north of Fort McMurray, one of the first places where humans put down roots in Alberta after the retreat of the glaciers. The quarry has been identified as the source of the sandstone tools that are found at hundreds of sites in northern Alberta and Saskatchewan, including spear points, knives, scrapers, stone flakes and micro-blades.

Right Seeking ancient tools at Fort Calgary in the Quarry of the Ancestors, Alberta, Canada.

Above A Neanderthal skull (*left*) is shown alongside that of a Cro-Magnon skull – an early *Homo sapiens* (*right*).

The gender division debate

It is understandable to think that the informational potential of the scanty remains of early human activity will be rapidly exhausted. What more could an archaeologist excavating a site with human remains have to say once the bones, flints and hearth debris have been dated and described? These tough robust things that endure as evidence of human activity when slighter, more fragile and more interesting materials rot and fade away, can seem unpromising as evidence for human thought and activity, yet, thanks to the ingenuity and creativity of archaeologists who think hard about the meaning of finds, that is exactly what they can be encouraged to yield.

One of the great debates in archaeology concerns the fate of the Neanderthals, who flourished in Europe 130,000 years ago but became extinct about 24,000 years ago. Theories to account for their demise include competition from our own species – *Homo sapiens* – perhaps including deliberate genocide on our part, and the lack of survival strategies to cope with the bitterly cold conditions of the last ice age, which drove Neanderthals to seek refuge in caves in southern Spain.

However, if cold weather is to blame, surely *Homo sapiens* faced exactly the same conditions? Why did we survive and not them? By thinking about this problem, Steven L. Kuhn and Mary C. Stiner of the University of Arizona have theorized that it was the division of labour by gender that gave modern humans an advantage over Neanderthals. The archaeologists noted that discarded animal bones found at Neanderthal sites show that their diets depended on large game. They also considered the presence of healed fractures on female and juvenile Neanderthal skeletons, suggesting that women and children shared the task of hunting game and were injured as a result. The food remains of *Homo sapiens* of the same period include bones from small animals and birds, as well as milling stones for grinding nuts and seeds. Women and children don't exhibit the same serious injures, and cave deposits include bone awls and needles used for making clothes and shelters. All of this is seen as evidence for the emergence of 'female' roles and crafts among Homo sapiens, allowing them to exploit the environment more efficiently and enjoy the advantages of co-operation and complementary roles for men, women and children.

Metalwork Finds

The metalwork that is found on archaeological sites is usually corroded and is often unidentifiable. Nevertheless, metalwork finds can still yield important information – but first they have to be subjected to conservation, specialist cleaning and analytical tests.

Above This hammered bronze disk from Ireland is typical of the 'Celtic' style.

Silver and gold are two of the more stable elements and are less subject to the oxidization that causes rust and corrosion in many other metals. Everyone who has ever come across precious metal during an excavation testifies to the special thrill of finding that tell-tale glint of sunlike colour in the ground that indicates gold coinage or jewellery. However, that experience is a rare one, and the metal that archaeologists routinely find is usually of a different order – more often an unpromising lump of rust or corrosion that hides the original shape of the object, which is only revealed when it has been X-rayed. Fortunately, modern X-ray equipment is quick and easy to use and is non-destructive, and so it is now routinely used in archaeological laboratories to analyse corroded metalwork before the objects are cleaned and conserved.

Humble metalwork

Metalwork from archaeological sites tends to be either very routine or very special. Particularly common types of metalwork include nails – used for every type of construction, from boxes to buildings – and parts of buckets and containers, horse harnesses, buckles, and belt fittings, as well as hobnails for boots and sandals.

However, even the functional and humble can have a surprising cultural significance. Archaeologists recently excavated one of the largest burial sites in north-east Cuba, at El Chorro de Maíta, which dates from the period immediately after the Spanish conquest of the island. In many of the graves, archaeologists found necklaces made of small metal tubes. Analysis revealed that these were brass aglets, from European clothing, used from the 15th century onward to prevent fraying on the ends of laces used to fasten clothes, such as doublets and hose, and shoes. Because gold was such a commonplace metal for the indigenous Cubans, they elevated functional European brass to the level of something precious and turned it into an ornament.

Early metallurgy

Perhaps because there is something magical about the transformation of ore into metal, it is often the case that some of the most spectacular finds of all are metal – and not just of gold. In many different cultures – European, African and Asian – bronze and iron have been used in spectacularly effective ways to create decorative objects. These are as varied as the engraved and enamelled mirrors of the Iron Age La Tène culture, the reliefs and scenes from courtly life of the bronzes from the Kingdom of Benin, in Africa, and the bronze bells and tripods of ancient China.

In the European Bronze Age, the magic of metal has been reflected in the deliberate destruction of costly metalwork, and its offering to the gods through deposition in rivers and pools. A celebrated example is a late Bronze-Age shield made from a sheet of bronze that was beaten into a circular shape, stamped with 29 concentric circles and decorated with rows of small bosses and raised ribs. The shield was found by Dr Ferris 'in a peat moss' in about 1780 at Lugtonridge, near Beith, in Aryshire, Scotland, along with five other similar shields (sadly all now lost), buried deep in the peat and arranged vertically in a ring. It is assumed that the shields were deposited in the bog as a ceremonial offering – and several holes had been punched through the sheet of bronze as a form of ritual 'killing' of the shield before it was placed in the boggy pool.

The Lugtonridge shield is by no means an isolated example; bogs, fens and pools, rivers and streams have yielded up an astonishing array of very

Below This example of the phenomenal Benin bronze work from West Africa (1440–1897), depicts the head of an Oba king.

Above A pair of gold earrings (*top*) and a gold hair ornament (*bottom*) were found in the Archer's grave.

fine metalwork, in the form of axes, shields, cups and cauldrons, suggesting that the makers of such complex and sophisticated objects felt they needed to give something back to the earth from whence the magic metal substance originally came.

Metals and trade

Typologies have long been established for many common metalwork types, as they have been for pottery. For example, the ubiquitous bronze brooches from Iron Age, Roman and early medieval sites that were used to fasten clothes together. Recent research has concentrated on analysing the metal to understand the range of alloy types employed and relate this to

Above A bronze urn at China's Forbidden City, Beijing. The palace was built by the Mongols from 1406–1420, and achieved its full splendour under the Ming dynasty. The palace name refers to the fact that occupants required the emperor's permission to leave.

brooch type and decoration. By mapping alloys to known sources of iron, copper, zinc, tin, aluminium, silicon, nickel, lead and other trace elements, such as mercury, arsenic, phosphorus and manganese, it is hoped that this will lead to identifying the location of the mines and of individual workshops.

What archaeologists already know is that the mastery of metalworking skills has led to power and status. This can be seen by studying the rise of civilizations, such as the ancient Etruscans, whose exploitation of the mineral wealth of the island of Elba and the Colline Metallifere (literally 'Metal-bearing hills') of Tuscany helped them dominate central Italy from 800BC until they were conquered by the Romans.

Amesbury Archer

The finds in the grave of the 'Amesbury Archer', discovered 5km/3 miles from Stonehenge, is the richest of any individual grave found in Great Britain from the Early Bronze Age (2,400–1,500BC). The archer was buried with two gold hair tresses, the oldest securely dated gold found in Britain (from about 2,400BC). Tools from the grave showed that he possessed metalworking skills and might have been regarded by his community as a man with magical powers, hence his special treatment in the grave.

Below An artist's impression of how the Amesbury Archer may have looked.

Left Metal detectors at shipwreck sites can reveal rare artefacts of great historical significance. These colonial Spanish silver coins were recovered from the *Whydah*, a ship that sunk off Cape Cod in 1717.

Pottery as Evidence of Everyday Life

In the debris of day-to-day life, archaeologists can find evidence for social and economic activity, symbols of thought, details about lifestyles, fashions, beliefs, agricultural practice and foods consumed, clothing, art, industry, allegiances, warfare and kinship — and this is a far from exhaustive list.

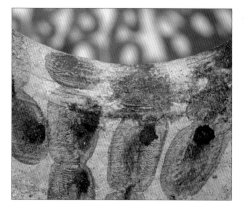

Above Finger marks made on a clay object are the remnants of work by a Roman potter.

Typically, the archaeologist is faced with describing unromantic holes in the ground, and explaining the patterns they make. Post holes and timber slots become houses of various shapes and internal arrangements. Ditches become drainage gullies, defensive enclosures and irrigation canals, associated with water scoops, ponds, wells, field boundaries and trackways. Pits become grain stores or refuse sites, and other types of evidence can be explained as industrial sites where pottery and iron making went on, quarrying sites where raw materials were extracted and worked, mills where materials such as grain or pigments were ground, butchery sites where animals were slaughtered and converted to meat, leather, horn or bone tools. This run-of-the-mill catalogue of basic human activities and site types is what makes up the majority of the archaeological record, with its evidence of the human struggle to survive.

The invention of pottery

Where the archaeologist can begin to get an insight into the life of ancient people beyond mundane subsistence is in the pottery record. Pottery is one of those inventions that is taken for granted and is assumed to have been with humans since the dawn of time, although the earliest clay objects found

so far consist of figurines, such as the so-called Venus of Dolní Vûstonice, a nude female figure dating to between 29,000 and 25,000BC.

The earliest pottery vessels come from Japan and have been dated by thermoluminescence to 11,000BC. China had pottery by 8,000BC and by 3,000BC ceramic vessels can be found everywhere in the world, either spread by trade and diffusion from eastern to western Asia, or invented independently, as is the case in North Africa during the 8th millennium BC and in South America during the 5th millennium BC.

Pottery from excavation

One of the most common forms of ancient material to be found surviving on any archaeological site is pottery. Excavation reports often contain pages

of drawings and descriptions of the different types of vessel, which the pottery specialist can reconstruct from diagnostic fragments, such as shard from a rim or base.

The technique is relatively straightforward because pottery typologies have been built up for just about all the known pottery types recovered from archaeological sites. The colour of the pot is one important clue, along with the character of its 'fabric', the material from which the vessel is made, as well as such inclusions as sand, grit, shell, or ground-up pottery.

The shape of a vessel can often be guessed by measuring the diameter of the rim or base along with the curvature of the body. An experienced pottery expert will often be able to date a piece of pottery at a glance, identify the vessel type (such as

Right Authentic sculpted earthenware from the Kanto Province of Japan has been dated to the Jomon period (14,000–4,000BC).

Above Some Japanese ceramicists have been designated 'Living National Treasures' in recognition of their efforts to revitalize and emulate the intricate craft of ancient dynasties.

cooking pot, storage jar, cremation urn or water jug) and say where it might have been made.

Daily life, fashions and trade

For the expert, identifying the pottery is only the starting point for an exploration of the wider meaning of the pottery assemblage from the site. The range of vessel types represented in that assemblage will tell an expert about the status and wealth of the people who lived there. For example, are these the basic cooking and storage pots of peasant life or specialized vessels with fine fabric and decoration associated with wealthier lifestyles? Are these the products of local pottery kilns, or are they exotic imports? Are they utilitarian in design, or decorated, and is the fabric coarse or fine? All these are potential clues to the quality of life of the owners, of the degree to which the site is linked into wider trading networks, of whether the site is part of the backwater or the main-stream of the prevailing fashions and trends in pottery.

The existence of coarse wear and fine wear side by side in these assemblages also warns experts not to interpret fine tablewares as evidence for a growing expertise in pot making – instead it can indicate differing usages. Up until the recent past, people often had a mix of pottery types in their homes. As well as fine pottery – such as the ubiquitous 'Willow pattern' wares found all over Europe, North America and the 'colonies' from the 19th century, they might also buy more functional wares, such as storage jars and cooking pots, from local potters, who sold their wares using itinerant pedlars, going from door to door.

Debris from a king?

A classic example of pottery as an indicator of status and trade is the case of Tintagel, in Cornwall, Great Britain. Major excavations undertaken by Ralegh Radford in the 1930s uncovered remains of 5th- to 6th-century buildings, where significant volumes of eastern Mediterranean and North African pottery suggested a site with trade links stretching to Constantinople, the capital and hub of the late Roman and early Byzantine world. Radford interpreted Tintagel as the site of either a Celtic monastery or the fortress of a wealthy and powerful king or tribal leader – reinforcing the popular (but archaeologically incorrect) belief that Tintagel is one possible location for the court of King Arthur and his Knights of the Round Table.

Above Fired pottery was found at a Bronze-Age Aegean site at Akrotiri, Greece.

Kiln sites

Pottery experts can pinpoint where a pot was made by examining the minerals in the fabric of the shard under a microscope and matching the clays and inclusions to known clay sources. Given the spectacular nature of Greek pottery, with its many pottery shapes and decorative motifs, it is not surprising that one of the main areas for this kind of work is Athens, where research institutes are mapping the main clay sources and kiln sites for Aegean pottery production back to the Early Bronze Age (or Early Helladic) period, which dates from 2800–2100BC. The results suggest a sophisticated knowledge of sources of clay suitable for ceramic production. By mapping the distribution of pottery around the islands from these kilns, important clues have been given to the far-ranging trade networks of the region, involving raw materials, such as tin, copper and charcoal, but also finished goods, such as bronze and ceramics.

Above These castle ruins at Tintagel, Cornwall, date to the 12th century, but lie on top of a 5th-century palace that has long been associated with the court of King Arthur, the fictional Camelot.

Pottery: the Key to Food Preparation

Pottery can tell archaeologists something about the owner's wealth, social status and trading links, but what about the food they contained? This is a question that a number of specialists will try to address as part of their study of the finds from the site.

Above Bread- and beer-making are depicted on an Egyptian 5th-dynasty tomb mural.

Some types of pottery can offer clues to the foods eaten in the past because their shape is very specific and reflects their function. Round-bottomed vessels, or vessels with short legs, were shaped like that so that they could be embedded in embers and ash, where the contents would slowly cook, whereas pottery and metal braziers have been found that are indicative of broiling or grilling over a barbecue and bakestones are indicative of flatbreads, bannocks, griddle cakes and pancakes, and domed clay ovens indicate the baking of raised loaves.

Lipid analysis

As well as vessel shape, the food residues trapped within the vessel or coating its surface can provide specific information. Since the early 1990s,

Left A beaker recovered from the grave of the Amesbury Archer, probably used in rituals involving beer.

specialists in biomolecular archaeology have been looking through their microscopes to search for ancient traces of blood, lipids (fats and fatty acids), proteins, carbohydrates and plant molecules, which survive on the surfaces and within the vessel walls of unglazed – and therefore porous – pottery.

One aim of this research is to seek the origins of foods that are known to be ancient. There is now evidence, for example, of cultured milk products – including yogurts, butter and cheese – all being produced as food for at least 8,000 years, perhaps as an accidental result of storing milk in bags made from sheep or goat stomachs. Bee-keeping and honey production is perhaps even older – milk and honey are among the first foodstuffs that are mentioned in the Bible.

Beer might also be an accidental discovery, as the by-product of bread-making. Beer residues have been found on a pottery vessel dating to 3500BC, which was found at the site of Godin Tepe in the Zagros Mountains of western Iran. Similar residues have been found in Bronze Age pottery (2100–1400BC) from northern Spain, but mixed with hemlock. This is a poisonous plant that ancient Greeks were forced to drink as a form of capital punishment.

However, the presence of hemlock in small amounts can also indicate ritual use. In small quantities hemlock can have an hallucinogenic effect without being toxic.

Food preservation

Butter- and cheese-making is one way of converting a food that deteriorates rapidly – milk – into forms that are stable and long lasting, which can ensure a food supply through the lean months of winter. Archaeologists know from bone assemblages that milk-producing animals are present in some quantity in most human cultures. However, for evidence of the specific conversion of raw milk into butter or cheese for longer term

Below A Neolithic clay dish from the Czech region of Moravia, known as 'spiral-meander' pottery due to the pattern in the clay and the culture that produced it. Used as drinking vessels, handles were later added to make them portable.

Above These Iron-Age storage pots, recovered from the Czech Republic, would have been used to store liquids (the smaller vessels in the foreground) and food (the larger vessels).

storage, they need to look for pottery types specific to that process. This includes strainers, which are vessels with holes in the base to allow liquid to drain away when milk separates into solid curds and liquid whey during cheese-making.

Because salt can preserve food, it was seen as a precious commodity. The methods people have used to obtain salt can leave distinctive archaeological evidence, such as in the form of salterns – shallow tanks or scoops in the ground where sea water is left to evaporate slowly, leaving crystalline salt behind. This evidence is also found in a type of pottery called briquetage, large shallow vessels in which sea water or brine from salt springs is boiled to evaporate the water, leaving the salt behind.

Salt mines in Austria

There is intriguing early evidence of salt-meat production on an industrial scale at the ancient Dürnberg salt mines in Austria, dating from 800BC, if not earlier. Here, a massive amount of pig bone has been found in association with the mine workings, suggesting that pigs were herded to the mines and slaughtered, then preserved on site using rock salt extracted from the mine. Maybe the reason for bringing the pigs to the mines rather than selling salt to farmers, who would salt their own animals, was to retain a monopoly over the precious commodity of salt.

The discovery and exploitation of the mines corresponds to the rise of the La Tène culture in central Europe, an Iron-Age culture that is renowned for the astonishing complexity, richness and intricacy of its geometrical art, manifested in jewellery and polished bronze mirrors. Some archaeologists have suggested that the grave goods found in La Tène burials indicate the rise of a princely class based on the monopoly over salted products.

Digging deep

The Iron-Age salt mines at Dürnberg, in Austria, Europe, are remarkable for the preservation of organic remains – the salinity is so concentrated there that destructive microbes cannot survive. This means that pieces of ancient clothing, discarded and lost by workers, have survived in the mines, as have their faeces, or coprolites, which can also be found in ancient cess pits or preserved in waterlogged sites. Careful examination in laboratory conditions has identified the parasites that our ancestors had, and the medicines that they took to rid themselves of afflictions. Wormwood bark and coriander seeds were found to be commonly used as purgatives.

Above Portrait of workers at the Dürnberg mine, the oldest salt mine in Europe.

Ancient Diets

Looking even further back into ancient diets, bones, lipids and isotopes can provide broad clues about the origins of food and drink staples. Direct evidence for diet comes from the numerous food bones that are usually found on archaeological sites.

Above Olives excavated at Pompeii, which survived the onslaught of lava and hot ash.

Food bones – the discarded bones of animals eaten by humans – suggest that our ancestors had a very varied diet and were willing to eat a much wider range of wild foods than we might now contemplate. In addition to domestic cattle, sheep, goat and pig bones, archaeologists have found wild red deer, boar, beaver, hare, heron, swan, plover, various types of duck and wildfowl, freshwater and sea fish, and even hedgehog, otter and badger at European sites dating from the last three millennia.

One of the ways that specialists can distinguish between bones that have formed part of a meal is by looking for butchery marks. Food bones are often found chopped up and fragmented, whereas animals hunted for fur but not for food (martens and wildcats, for example) occur as complete skeletons, being discarded whole after skinning and regarded as having no food value.

Food or medicine?

No doubt some of these animals were eaten experimentally, or in extremis, when poverty or deep winter offered no alternative source of food. Archaeologists also know that some foods were eaten for medicinal purposes. Beavers, for example, were driven to extinction in Europe mainly because the salicylin contained in their scent glands was a staple of medicine into the 19th century, used to relieve pain and fever and to treat inflammatory conditions, such as arthritis and rheumatism, which was only superseded with the discovery of aspirin. This association between the beavers' favourite food (willow twigs) and pain relief was made in the ancient past and was certainly known to the 5th century BC physician, Hypocrites, who stated that the bitter liquid extracted from soaking willow bark could ease aches and pains and reduce fevers.

Shopping lists

Written records can also help archaeologists understand ancient diets. A remarkable cache of writing tablets found on Hadrian's Wall, the Roman frontier between Britain and the land of the 'barbarians', to the north in Scotland, has revealed shopping lists and household inventories. The soldiers garrisoned there in the 1st and 2nd centuries AD enjoyed home-brewed beer and wine imported from Spain and Italy, some of which was sweetened with honey or flavoured with spices, including anise, caraway and lovage.

Samples from waterlogged pits at Hadrian's Wall shows that the military diet included figs, grapes, cherries, blackberries, apples, pears, raspberries and strawberries and even astringent fruits such as elderberries and sloes.

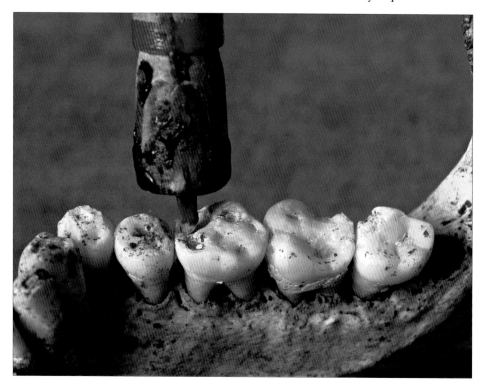

Left Adult teeth found at the site of Mehrgahr in Pakistan contain drilled holes and are evidence of the earliest known practice of dentistry. Archaeologists believe the holes were made 9,000 years ago to ease toothache using a tiny stone blade like the one shown in this reconstruction.

Olive and date stones, or pits, are commonly found, as are hazelnuts, along with peas, beans, lentils, beets and turnips – and plenty of seeds from nettle, suggesting that nettle soup was a part of the soldiers' diet.

Trade and imports

Some of these foods were clearly traded and carried long distances, because although the late Iron Age and Roman period was one of warm dry weather, with grapes and figs being cultivated in northern Europe, dates and olives from Asia must have been transported long distances by land and sea, as were some of the spices found in ancient deposits that can only have come from Asia via the spice routes – black pepper, for example, which turns up at Hadrian's Wall along with less exotic herbs, such as coriander, poppy seed, fennel and dill.

Some sense of the importance of pepper in the ancient diet can be gauged by the recipes in the oldest complete cookbook in possession. Called *De Re Coquinaria* (On Culinary Matters), it is usually attributed to a Roman author called Apicius, but it is more probably a compilation of recipes by several people. Pepper was used in 349 of the 468 recipes in the book, including dormice stuffed with pepper and pine nuts. The pepper and spice trade survived the collapse of the western Roman Empire and, pepper in the medieval period carried associations of ancient luxury and civility.

Isotopes in teeth and bones

Reaching even further back into time, archaeological scientists have begun examining ancient bone collagen in an attempt to understand ancient diets as far back as the Neolithic in Europe (prior to 3000BC). Measuring the ratios of nitrogen to carbon to sulphur isotopes in the collagen cannot tell scientists precisely what people ate, but it can be used to distinguish groups of people with a plant-rich, meat-rich, marine-rich or omnivorous diet. Archaeologists hope eventually to be able to pinpoint the rise of diets based

Right This Roman painting shows the contents of a fishmonger's shop as it would have appeared to customers in the 1st century AD, with squid, crab and bream for sale.

on domesticated animals and plants rather than wild foods, and perhaps to distinguish from the isotopes in tooth enamel what kind of minerals they ingested in drinking water in their childhood, and hence whether they are local people, or migrants to the region in which they spent the remainder of their years and were buried.

Above The excavation of the olive oil processing area at Tell es Sa'idiyeh, Jordan. This early Bronze-Age industrial complex, a hub for passing trade, was destroyed by fire around 2750BC, leaving archaeologists a wealth of charred organic remains to examine and date.

An ancient trading crossroads

Fieldwork can help archaeologists understand how far back in time some staples go. Excavations at Tell es Sa'idiyeh, in central Jordan, sits above the crossroads of two major trade routes among fertile agricultural land. This was the site of a prosperous city in 2900BC, and at that early age there is evidence of areas being set aside for olive oil production and storage, wine-making and textile preparation on an industrial scale, showing that the inhabitants were producing goods for trade.

A fire that swept through part of the city left behind a rich variety of charred plant material. Scientific study of the charred remains shows that the everyday ingredients of the Early Bronze Age diet were wheat and barley, lentils, chickpeas and fava beans, along with grapes, figs, olives and pomegranates, some of which were eaten fresh and some of which were dried to produce raisins and dried figs. What is remarkable about this list of staples is the extent to which it continues to underlie the modern diet of the region, suggesting that in matters of food, people are relatively conservative.

Analysing Human Remains

The analysis of human remains is an exciting field that is branching into many directions, from the study of disease to understanding the ancient beliefs and rituals that led to the building of striking monuments. Many archaeological reports have substantial sections of human remains.

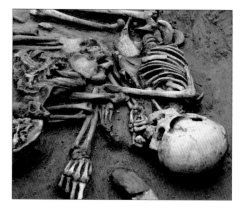

Above A complete skeleton of an old man lies in situ in its place of burial.

Human bodies can turn up virtually anywhere. Ancient burial mounds, tombs and cemeteries are one of the most common forms of monument to survive, and they have long been a focus of archaeological curiosity, from the earliest days of antiquarian digging.

Bones and diseases

Many bone specialists trained as doctors, so they are able to look at bones with professional eyes and can diagnose the many injuries and diseases to which humans were – and still are – vulnerable – not only battle wounds and the conditions of old age, but more esoteric complaints, such as gout, a condition that is erroneously associated with a rich diet and a fondness for after-dinner port. A high

incidence of gout was found in Romano–British people excavated from a cemetery in Cirencester, Gloucestershire. One theory is that the ingestion of lead could be a factor in the onset of gout, and Romans were exposed to lead through the pipes that supplied their water and through the cooking vessels used to prepare a sweetener called defrutum, made by boiling grape juice to form a syrup. However, Roman citizens all over the Roman Empire faced the same exposure to lead, so osteo-archaeologists (those who specialize in bone) now think gout could be related to the high levels of calcium in the local limestone-filtered water rather than a fondness for the yet-to-be-invented fortified wine.

The evidence of poor diet, lacking in essential vitamins and minerals, can be seen in the bone and teeth deformations associated with rickets and scurvy, but just as often archaeologists find indications of indulgence and dietary excess, and it is interesting to see which parts of the population are healthy and which are the gluttons. A study published in 2004 revealed, for example, that obesity was five times more prevalent among monks than among their secular contemporaries, including wealthy merchants or courtiers. Although gluttony is one of the Seven Deadly Sins, and is in direct contravention of the Rule of

Below Mass burial sites usually indicate a large, sudden loss of life due to war or disease.

Below An infant crouch burial in the Boscombe Down Roman cemetery, UK.

Grave goods

Even if archaeologists don't fully understand ancient ritual and religion, they know that it is responsible for some of our most enduring monuments – from pyramids and the tomb of Tutankhamun, to the terracotta warriors of the Chinese Emperor Xing, to the stone circles of Europe and the temples of southern America. Respect for the dead is not unique to *Homo sapiens*: Neanderthal graves have been found in Iraq dating back 80,000 years, in which flowers have been placed in the grave of the deceased, as well as grave goods, such as food, in the form of the bones of bison and auroch, stone tools and pieces of ochre pigment.

Above and left Farming and warfare are reflected in the sickle and spears found in the graves of ancient Greeks during the excavation of a 5th to 3rd century BC site at Édessa, in Macedonia. It is believed that the pottery might have contained food for the deceased on their journey to the afterlife.

St Benedict, which states that 'there is nothing so opposed to Christian life as overeating', archaeologists found numerous cases of medical conditions triggered by a fat-rich diet. For example, the bone condition known as diffuse idiopathic skeletal hyperostosis (DISH, or Forestier's disease), which is commonly associated with type 2 (late onset) diabetes, caused by a diet rich in suet, lard and butter.

Normal and deviant burials

The manner in which the dead are buried reveals a lot about ancient beliefs. Burial practice can be specific to a culture, such as the mummification of the ancient Egyptians, the east to west orientation of Christian burial, or the coin in the mouth that typifies Roman burial custom (to pay the ferryman who takes the spirit across the River Hades).

Archaeologists are far from understanding the meaning of much burial practice, especially when it departs from normal practice. For example, the graves of the Lapita people, the first settlers of the western Pacific, all contain headless skeletons, and some graves had cone shell rings in lieu of the skulls, indicating that the graves were reopened after burial and the heads removed. Sometimes the heads are separately buried nearby and sometimes they are moved to other graves. In one grave, three skulls were found on a man's chest – none of the skulls were his.

Although this treatment of skulls was normal practice for the Lapita people, it would be unusual in a European context – which is why the 30 Roman skeletons found recently in York, England, with their heads

removed and placed between their knees, on their chests or by their feet is a mystery.

Even more unusual is the mass grave at Evreux, in Normandy, France, found in 2006. It dates from the 3rd century, and bones of some 40 people have been deliberately mixed with the remains of 100 horses. Normally, graves of this period are organized and orderly, but this strange example defies explanation. In such cases, archaeologists often use the word 'ritual' to describe what they do not understand.

Below and left Archaeologists draw human remains and grave goods at a Lapita burial site. Skulls were typically removed from the skeletons and placed in a ceremonial container (*left*).

The Information in our Genes

Today's archaeological headlines are usually dominated by studies that involve extracting genetic material from bone. These archaeologists are looking for diagnostic genes that can help answer big questions about human origins and the peopling of the world.

Above Forensic scientists examining human bones look first for obvious signs of trauma.

Whenever human remains are found today, the director of the site will always bear in mind the potential information that can be found by doing a DNA study. One example that caught the popular imagination occurred in the late 1990s, when DNA was extracted from a tooth belonging to Cheddar Man – the oldest complete human skeleton yet found in England.

Migration or diffusion?

Cheddar Man was found in Gough's Cave in Cheddar Gorge, Somerset, and dates back to 7150BC. The DNA from his tooth was compared with DNA from saliva taken from people living in the village today. The comparison turned up two exact matches – both among local schoolchildren – and there is one very close match, with someone who by coincidence turned out to be a history teacher.

The serious archaeological issue behind this discovery was the question that has preoccupied archaeologists for decades. How stable have human populations been in the past, and is cultural innovation the result of migration or diffusion – of people moving into new territories and bringing ideas with them, or of ideas spreading through the network of contacts that exist between stable populations? One hundred years ago, when war and conquest was part of the diet fed to school pupils as a part of the national history, it was natural to favour the idea that conquerors brought innovation. However, DNA studies have suggested different answers. In the Cheddar example, there isn't a lot of evidence in the genetic record for foreign genes, showing that the populations have remained largely stable for thousands of years.

The big picture

This large view of populations is always open to small-scale exceptions, and one excavation can easily produce a thought-provoking result. Current archaeological theory suggests that human beings are all derived from migrants who began to spread out of eastern Africa about 100,000 years ago. Travelling along coastal routes and feeding on marine species, these emigrants spread to the rest of the world, reaching Asia and Australia at least 50,000 years ago, replacing other hominids that had spread across the world as a result of earlier migrations, such as the Neanderthals and Java and Peking man.

This theory has been based on two key assumptions. One is the so-called genetic clock, which is based on the finding that genes will mutate at a fairly regular rate, and this is the basis for the dating of the various migrations. The other assumption is the so-called genetic gateway, which says that when a population moves on to a new location (for example, from Siberia to North America) the gene pool of that population will be a subset of the gene pool of the parent population, and that

Above The fossilized cranium of the *Homo erectus* specimen known as 'Java Man' was discovered in 1969 in Indonesia.

Left The indigenous people of Papua New Guinea's Trobriand Islands bury their dead in open-air cemeteries, so when archaeologists found burials from around AD1500 inside caves (for example at Selai Cave, shown here), they suspected migration by Polynesians, arriving in Melanesia from the east, bringing a different burial practice. Reflecting this migration, the physical appearance and culture of the Trobriand Islands people today is more Polynesian than Melanesian in character.

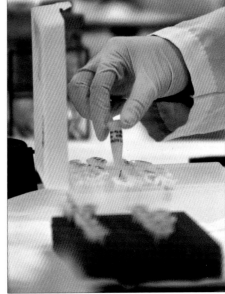

interbreeding in the new population will create a new gene pool with different characteristics from the parent population.

Above Archaeologists examine skulls belonging to human ancestors at the Laboratory of Prehistory in Nice, France.

Above A sample phial containing human DNA is selected for analysis at a laboratory specializing in human evidence.

Exceptions from the norm

As with much archaeology, specialists in ancient DNA seek to establish a body of data to describe what is normal or typical, then once the mainstream pattern is understood, they then begin to look for the exceptions – the telltale details that depart from the norm and require explanation.

For example, theories have been published recently to explain what appears to be a pattern of genetic differences between the western and eastern halves of Britain. Such differences have been detected in the archaeological record, and were once believed to be the result of continental invaders – Romans, Saxons, Angles and later Vikings. It has been thought that these invaders pushed the native British population westward into what is now Wales, Cornwall and western Scotland. Now a new, more complex picture is emerging of a post ice-age migration of genetically distinct people from northern Spain into the western side of Britain up the Atlantic and of a similar migration of genetically distinct people from the Germanic near Continent – hence the east-west divide might be 13,000 years old, rather than a recent and historic event.

Above Cerveteri, near Rome, is famed for its well-preserved ancient Etruscan tombs.

The origin of the mysterious Etruscans

The Etruscan civilization in Italy has long been a mystery, but the question of where the ancient Etruscans came from might have been solved through two separate genetic studies. The first looked at the genes of cattle in north, south and central Italy. Specialists in animal genetics have found that Tuscan white cattle are genetically close to Near Eastern cows, whereas there was no genetic convergence between cows from the north and south of Italy and those from the Near East. If correct, this confirms the hypothesis of an eastern origin for the Etruscans, first claimed by the classic historians Herodotus and Thucydides.

A second study involved taking genetic samples from three present-day Tuscan populations living in Murlo, Volterra and Casentino, chosen because they are three of the most archaeologically important Etruscan sites in a region that is known for having Etruscan-derived placenames and its own local dialect. The Tuscan samples were taken from individuals who had lived in the area for at least three generations, and whose surnames were unique to the region. These DNA samples were compared with samples taken from males living in northern Italy, the southern Balkans, the island of Lemnos in Greece, the Italian islands of Sicily and Sardinia and from several modern Turkish and Middle-Eastern populations. The scientists found that the Tuscan and Turkish samples were a close match and that both were different from the other Italian samples. The results reinforce the cattle gene study, reinforcing the idea that the ancient Etruscans migrated to Tuscany from the Near East.

Preparing the Publication and the Archive

Once all this information has been assembled in the form of a series of specialist reports, it is the director's task to weave them into a narrative that – along with supporting pictures, drawings and data – can be published so that other archaeologists can learn from what has been found at the site.

Above Compiling the results of an excavation is very complex when the data is this extensive.

Traditionally, the results of an excavation are published as a report in an archaeological journal or as a book. Many archaeologists still aspire to publish their excavations in this way, because publication in book or journal form is perceived as having a certain status. This is reinforced by the fact that many university funding systems assess the quality and productivity of their research staff on the basis of the books they write and the papers they publish in leading international journals, and review this regularly.

However, the volume of data being generated by modern archaeology is so great that the idea of publishing a complete record of the site is being challenged as the norm for archaeological report writing. Increasingly,

archaeologists are being encouraged to think of the results of an excavation in terms of 'data' and 'synthesis'.

By data, archaeologists mean the record of what was found – the site matrix and context record sheets, the plans, sections and photographs, and the artefacts and ecofacts, along with records, drawings and the reports of specialists identifying, describing and dating those finds. Synthesis means an interpretative narrative, which seeks to explain the meaning of the data – what it represents in terms of a chronological sequence of human events and activities at the site.

Not all archaeologists accept the validity of this separation of raw data from its explanation. Others disagree about which is more important. Some archaeologists argue that the interpretation is subjective and will soon be superseded by new thinking, and so should form only a small part of any report. They argue that the data takes

priority and should be published in full so that it is accessible to other archaeologists who can study it and form their own views about what it means. The implication of this position is that the data is capable of multiple interpretations, all of which might be equally valid until tested by debate at conferences and in teaching seminars or by further excavation and research.

Using digital data

This debate would have reached a stalemate but for the advent of digital technologies that enable excavation data to be presented in ways that printed publications cannot emulate. Computer-based graphics and design programmes now allow the data from excavations to be represented in three dimensions. Instead of wasting words in tedious descriptions of the site, the measurements that were recorded on site can be fed into computer-aided design (CAD) software that presents the data visually, in three dimensions, showing the stratigraphy and the precise find spot of every artefact or soil sample. By recording this data as a series of layers, and by using colours and shading, the site can effectively be brought back to life.

What is more, archaeologists who then study the material can subsequently make their own enquiries of the data and explore it in ways that might not have been in the mind of the original excavator. For example, someone interested in the archaeology of

Below and below right Reported finds, such as this coffin 'furniture' (*left*) and Saxon comb made of antler (*right*), are described, dated and placed in their historical context.

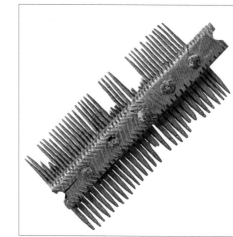

Left Many archaeologists now use design software to produce reports, although complex graphics may be added by a CAD specialist.

gender might look at the results of a cemetery excavation and analyse the finds in a number of ways, looking to see if any differences between men and women can be discerned in the positioning of graves within the cemetery – are there, perhaps, separate areas for man and women? Or the archaeologist may examine the objects placed in their graves – do keys, brooches, scissors, shears or combs distinguish female burials, and knifes, shields and hobnail shoes distinguish men, and what might it mean if a man is found buried with keys? And are there any skeletal differences evident that could be the result of differences between female and male diets, activities or susceptibility to disease?

Producing a digital report

In the case of digital publishing, some of the work of preparing the publication will require someone with expertise in computer-aided design, database design and management, as well as Relational or Geographical Information Systems (GIS) and graphics packages for manipulating drawings and photographs.

In larger commercial exaction units, the management of all of these activities might fall to a professional managing editor, whose responsibilities include finding a publisher and negotiating terms, applying for grants to help with the cost of the publication and handling the marketing, sales and distribution of the report. However, it often falls to the site director to undertake all of these tasks.

Conservation and archiving

In addition to publishing skills, a career in archaeology can also be combined with work in conservation, record keeping, archiving and information management. Once such work was relatively limited in scope: archaeological archivists would spend their days in dark basements, cleaning

Below When presenting the results of an excavation as a publication or lecture, many archaeologists will now try to include images of how the environment may have looked.

Why keep the archive?

Storing excavation material is expensive and it is tempting to ask why bother? Digital technology allows for creating virtual versions of the evidence we destroy. However, when new, unexpected technological and scientific developments come along, a virtual record will not help. The revolution in understanding human origins has come about because of our ability to extract DNA from fossilized bones dug up 100 years ago. If they hadn't been kept, it would be necessary to search for new material to dig up and test. In the case of a piece of wood excavated in 1945 from a Mesolithic site in Yorkshire, England, and saved in a glass jar in the Department of Archaeology in Cambridge, England, 60 years later an archaeologist recognized the strange markings on the wood as early evidence for the existence of beavers in post-ice age Britain.

objects, labelling them, conserving them and guarding them against harm – which some of them interpreted as meaning that nobody else should be allowed to touch them.

In recent times, however, more progressive organizations actively promote their archives as teaching and learning resources, and people are encouraged to take full advantage of them. When faced with the problem of storing the vast amounts of material that have been excavated in London, England, over the last 100 years, the Museum of London Archaeology Service set up the innovative London Archaeological Archive Resource Centre (www.museumoflondon.org. uk/laarc/new/default.asp) as a place where anyone can study the primary records and finds. Similar public facilities exist at Colonial Williamsburg, in the United States, for example, and at many other university archives around the world, helping to make archaeology more accessible.

Case Study: the Aegean Dendrochronology Project

Above Volcanic landscape on the Greek island of Thera (known also as Santorini) showing pumice covering the (prior) Minoan land surface. The dating of this event is pivotal to chronologies of the region.

One good example of the way that excavation directors and specialists can work together has been demonstrated by the Aegean Dendrochronology Project. Finds from individual excavation sites have been amalgamated to build up a database of material of value to everyone working in the region.

The Aegean Sea, which separates the mainlands of Greece and Turkey, is remarkable for its archeologically rich islands, bearing testimony to some of the world's earliest civilizations. It is the focus of numerous excavations and research projects every year.

Archaeologists working in the region know that if they find wood that can be dated using dendrochronology, or tree-ring dating, they need look no further for specialist help than the Malcolm and Carolyn Wiener Laboratory for Aegean and Near Eastern Dendrochronology, based at Cornell University, in the United States. This laboratory is home to the Aegean Dendrochronology Project, founded by Peter Ian Kuniholm, and now directed by Sturt Manning. The project team has spent three decades scouring sites in the Aegean (and from Italy to the Near East region) for samples of ancient wood to try to create a tree-ring sequence for the last 10,000 years of human and environmental history. The aim is to provide a dating method for the study of history and prehistory in the Aegean that is so accurate that it can date ancient timbers to the precise year in which they were cut down and used as construction material.

The Port of Theodosius

During the 2006 and 2007 seasons the laboratory has been busy in Istanbul, where the construction of a new railway tunnel beneath the Bosporus, linking Europe and Asia, has led to the discovery of a series of harbours dubbed the 'Port of Theodosius', dating from the reign of Emperor Theodosius in AD408. Archaeologists in Istanbul, led by Metin Gokcay, have found a church, a gated entrance to the city and several dozen sunken ships, as well as a series of stone- and timber-built harbours on a huge site that is four city blocks long by three wide. Work on some of the ships is in collaboration with Dr Cemal Pulak, of Texas A&M University and the Institute of Nautical Archaeology. The Istanbul archaeologists called in the Cornell Laboratory (Kuhiholm and group in 2006; Manning and group in 2007), who took samples across this vast site from

Left Sampling oak timbers at the Yenikapi site, Istanbul Harbour, Turkey.

most of the many timber pilings from a series of 4th- to 19th-century piers or docks and structures. Some samples and structures have already been dendro-dated as a result and, critically, some timbers belong to a key 4th- to 7th-century period – which the Aegean Dendrochronology Project needed to fill in the 'Roman Gap' in its sequence, and which may then in the future permit exact dendro-dating in Byzantine to Roman contexts in the region.

The more than 500 samples that the Cornell Laboratory teams have collected to establish the phasing of the various construction projects in the harbour will be added to a huge database of more than 40,000 existing wood samples that comprise the raw data for the Aegean master sequence.

The eruption of Thera

Apart from the value of the project as a crucial resource for dating Aegean and west Asian sites, the project can also pinpoint key environmental events by looking for patterns or signs that indicate vegetation under stress. One such event that had a major impact on the whole world's environment was the eruption of the volcano on the Aegean island of Thera (also known as Santorini); debris or evidence of the eruption has been found as far away as China, Greenland and the United

States. Dating the event would provide a marker, like the burial of Pompeii, for dating excavated sites in the region and for aligning Aegean, Egyptian, Cypriot and Asian chronology, however, the precise date for the eruption has proved hard to pin down.

Traditionally, the event has been dated to about 1500BC, based on similarities between pottery found buried in the volcanic ash in Akrotiri, a town on Thera destroyed by the blast, with similar styles of pottery in the rest of the Aegean, and the correlation of these styles with exchanges of Aegean/Egyptian objects and influences against the historical dates for the Egyptian kings of the New Kingdom period.

In 2006, Sturt Manning and his team rewrote ancient history by arguing that the eruption occurred 100 years earlier, in 1660–1613BC. To reach this conclusion, Manning and his colleagues analysed 127 tree-ring samples and seeds from Santorini, Crete, Rhodes and Turkey, testing them by radiocarbon dating and tree-ring analysis.

Coincidentally, the Cornell results were reinforced by a separate dendrochronology and radiocarbon study, led by Danish geologist Walter Friedrich, which dated an olive branch severed during the Santorini eruption and arrived independently at a late 17th-century BC date.

Rethinking the region's archeaology

The two sets of findings mean a shift of the dates for the Aegean civilization and its cultures and a new timeline that places a number of events earlier than previously thought, including the formation and high point of the New Palace period on Crete, the Shaft Grave period on the Greek mainland, and the Middle to late Cypriot period on Cyprus. The re-dating of the eruption also raises a number of questions about previously hypothesized dates and associations, and about the precise trading relationships and influences of one culture on another, with major ramifications for the archaeology and art history of the region.

Above Timber samples are analysed at the Cornell Tree-Ring Laboratory. The project has now amassed some 10 million separate samples, providing chronologies for more than 9,000 years.

Sturt Manning has said the results 'call for a critical rethinking of hypotheses that have stood for nearly a century... the earlier chronology would frame a different context, and a longer era, for the very genesis of Western civilization. The 17th century BC may become a very important period'.

Above Core samples are taken from a timbered house on the island of Crete.

Above Tree-ring samples from Cyprus contain vital information about the Santorini eruption.

CHRONOLOGIES

Until the mid-19th century, people only had a vague sense of the ancient past, derived mainly from the Bible, the epics of Homer, and the classical Greek and Latin authors, such as Thucydides and Herodotus, two of the first historians to write down the stories of past deeds and battles that had been hitherto handed down by word of mouth. This changed about 150 years ago with the development of scientific archaeological techniques borrowed in part from geology. Antiquarians did not suddenly become archaeologists overnight, and there were (and remain) religious objections to the new time frames that have emerged, but little by little the study of ancient bones and stone tools has given new insights into the origins of the human species and our development and interaction with the environment. This chapter explains in broad terms what archaeologists have learned over these last 150 years, and what they currently think about human origins and the development of world civilizations.

Opposite Passages linking houses of a Neolithic village at Skara Brae, Orkney Islands, occupied 3100–2500BC.

Above Archaeologists still have much to learn about the construction of megalithic Stonehenge, on Salisbury Plain, Britain.

Above Hieroglyphs and stone reliefs in The Valley of the Kings show the extraordinary craftmanship of ancient Egypt.

Above Machu Picchu – often referred to as the 'Lost City of the Incas' – was once the seat of a great emperor.

Defining the Ages

Much prehistoric archaeology is still based on the three-age system that divides prehistory into three main periods — the Stone Age, Bronze Age and Iron Age. However, the relevance of this framework to ancient civilizations outside of Europe is disputed territory.

Above Can ancient cultures, like that of Cambodia, be classified on the basis of simple materials?

The three-age chronology was first proposed by Nicholas Mahudel (1704–47), who observed from his excavation of multi-period burial mounds that bronze tools were found in the lower and earlier burials and iron in the later upper layers. He deduced that stone tools were easier to produce and, therefore, likely to be earlier, and he was one of the first antiquaries to argue convincingly that shaped flints were the work of human activity and not some form of fossil.

Mahudel's book *Three Successive Ages of Stone, Bronze, and Iron* (1734) was ahead of its time and only in the early decades of the 19th century did the three-age chronology become an accepted classification tool, when it was adopted by Christian Jürgensen Thomsen, founder of the Royal (now National) Museum of Denmark as the basis for classifying artefacts in the collection. Thomsen tends to get the credit for the idea, because he, and his protégé, Jens Jacob Worsaae, were such evangelists for the 'Copenhagen arrangement', writing books and giving lectures to learned societies all over Europe.

Growing complexity

Latin and Greek were used as universal languages for scientific communication in the 19th century, so the Old and New Stone Age subdivisions were called the Palaeolithic and the Neolithic when the British banker John

Right John Lubbock, a close acquaintance of Charles Darwin, was the first to publicly subdivide the Stone Age into new ('Neolithic') and old ('Palaeolithic') eras.

Lubbock (1834–1913), later Lord Avebury, first proposed these subdivisons in his book *Prehistoric Times* (1865), the first being characterized by simple all-purpose tools, such as axes, clubs and scrapers, and the later period by specialized stone tools, including chisels and reaping hooks. Recognition in the 1930s of a distinctive Middle Stone Age period, characterized by arrowheads and spear points, led to the naming of the Middle Stone Age, or Mesolithic.

This simple subdivision then took on greater and greater complexity over succeeding decades, as archaeologists began to realize that there were other toolmaking technologies intermediate between the three big subdivisions. Thus the Copper Age (also known as the Chalcolithic, from the Greek for 'copper stone') has since been added to the system as an intermediate phase

in the early use of metal tools between the Stone and Bronze Ages, and key stages within each age are now marked by further subdivisions into early, middle and late periods. Not all archaeologists agree with such rigid slices of time, and some argue endlessly about the precise point at which one period ends and another begins — or whether there is any fundamental difference between the Late Neolithic and the early Bronze Age (the term 'LaNeBrA' has been coined to describe this critical transition).

Below This Olmec statue dates from the Formative period (*c.* 600BC) in Mexico. The Olmecs were a precursor of the great Mesoamerican civilizations.

Old World vs New World

With the spread of archaeological research from Europe to other parts of the world, the universality of the three- (or four-) age system began to be questioned. It provided a good framework for European prehistory, but technology has never developed beyond the Stone Age in some parts of the world, while in other parts, technology went from the Stone to the Iron Ages with no Copper or Bronze Ages. In some parts of Asia, iron technology predated bronze, while ceramics, another key technology, vary in predating and postdating the metal phases. And where, some archaeologists ask, does wood, a material of importance to all societies, feature in all of this?

To complicate matters further, the duration of each phase varies from one part of the world to another. Dating each of these phases is a science in itself (*see* Radiocarbon Dating), but in some places the switch from one innovative metal technology (copper) to another (bronze) is fast, and in some cases there are long periods of conservatism. Neither is each phase exclusive: metal objects were made and used in the Neolithic, iron was made and used in the Bronze Age and bronze continued to be used in the Iron Age and beyond (in jewellery and coinage, for example).

Some archaeologists have argued that the three-age system has now outlived its usefulness. In the United States, the three-age system is recognized as having a value for Old World archaeology, but for the New World, a different five-stage framework was proposed in 1958 by Gordon Willey and Philip Phillips – the Lithic stage (hunting), the Archaic stage (gathering of wild resources), the Formative stage (early agriculture), the Classic stage (early civilizations) and the Post-Classic stage (later pre-Hispanic civilizations). Others have argued that we need to think in terms of cultures – the assemblages of tool types and other objects that distinguish one group of people living in a particular region from another – rather than the mechanistic technology of one tool type.

However, the system is still used because cultures do have something in common that enables them to be grouped according to tool type. These big archaeological ages also coincide with geological time systems and periods of glacial and climate change.

Above The 4th-century BC Ficoroni Cist (or cremation urn), decorated with mythical figures, shows the astonishing skill of Etruscan metal-workers during the European Bronze Age.

Below Traditional practices in which materials such as wood, ropes and woven leaves are utilized still survive in many parts of the world, demonstrating the difficulty in defining and separating archaeological periods. This woman uses a shoulder yoke in modern-day Burma.

The Earliest Humans

*Darwin's theory of evolution changed our perception of prehistory.
However, many questions remained unanswered until the advent of scientific
dating techniques in the post-war period, now supplemented by the study
of DNA, which have afforded accurate dating to early human remains.*

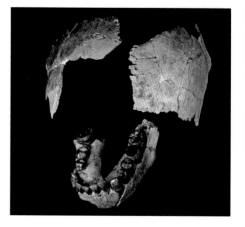

Above These *Homo habilis* skull bones were found in Olduvai Gorge, Tanzinia in 1960. They are estimated to be 1.75 million years old.

In the first half of the 19th century, knowledge gained from the emerging science of geology led to the growing awareness that the world was much older than the chronology worked out by James Ussher (1581–1656), the Anglican Archbishop of Armagh (now in Northern Ireland), who deduced from events and genealogies in the Bible that the earth was created on Sunday 23 October 4004BC.

Darwin's theory (published in 1859) that life forms are continually evolving in response to environmental stimuli then led to the idea that the human species was not created fully formed, but had evolved through potentially many different earlier stages of life. In 1863 Thomas Huxley (1825–95), a biologist and advocate of Darwin's theory of evolution, demonstrated the close similarities between the skulls and anatomy of humans and gorillas – attracting the derisory question from Archbishop Samuel Wilberforce of whether 'it was through his grandfather or grandmother that he claimed descent from a monkey.'

How accurate Huxley was in his deductions has only been proven in the 1960s, with the sequencing of primate and human genes to create a family tree that shows the hominid development from the early primates of 60 million years ago to the modern humans of today (the term 'hominid' includes apes and humans, whereas the term 'hominin' refers to the human lineage, including chimpanzees). The search for further evidence of human ancestry continues because there are many gaps still to be filled in the human family tree. This work is focused in areas of the world that are of the right geological time period to yield finds of fossil bones – in the Eastern Rift Valley of east Africa, in South Africa and in north African countries, such as Libya and Morocco.

Physical attributes

Until recently the study of human evolution was based almost exclusively on examining the physical attributes of skulls and skeletal material, much like archaeologists classify pots and metal-work into typologies. Before the advent of scientific dating techniques, people made assumptions about the chronology based on stratigraphy and on a simplistic interpretation of

Darwinian evolution, which saw adaptation as moving always from crude to sophisticated, from primitive to modern. In the case of skeletal remains, this led to some odd theories mixed up with ideas about racial superiority. In the 19th century, for example, it was commonly held that people could be classified as primitive or superior depending on whether they had rounded or elongated skulls.

What helped to put the study of human origins on a more scientific basis in the 1960s was the development

Above Thomas Huxley publicly advocated Darwinism against some of the most important theorists of 19th-century England. He coined the term 'agnostic', based on his own beliefs.

Above Archaeologists look for human evidence at Fejej in Ethiopia – a site that is currently recognized as the oldest human encampment in the world.

present day

4 million years ago

Above There is much interest in how our ancestors may have looked. This illustration shows the evolution of hominids from our distant ape-like ancestors through three groups of species, each one indicated by a different coloured line, to *Homo sapiens*.

of potassium-argon dating. This measures the ratios of the isotopes potassium 40 and argon 40 in the volcanic rocks or sediments in which the fossil bones are found, and is based on the fact that potassium 40 decays to form argon 40 at a steady rate. Added to this, microbiologists have discovered that DNA, the genetic material present in all living cells, is constantly mutating, and does so at a steady rate, serving as a genetic clock that enables scientists to calculate the likely dates of key stages in hominid development.

Our earliest ancestors

A consensus has developed over the core dates and developments that mark human evolution. Genetic scientists estimate that the split between hominids and apes occurred ten to eight million years ago. The discovery of the six- to seven-million year-old skull of *Sahelanthropus tchadensis* in the Djurab desert in northern Chad in 2002 takes archaeologists close to the point of human origin. This skull has a chimpanzee-like braincase but the flat face, prominent brow ridges and small teeth of a hominid.

Before that discovery, the oldest known hominid was the six-million-year-old *Orrorin tugenensis*, a bipedal

ape (using feet instead of knuckles and feet to bear the skeleton's weight). One challenge facing archaeologists is to identify when bipedalism occurred, marking the evolution from tree-dwelling to ground-dwelling hominids. Within the human family tree, the Australopithecines (literally 'Southern ape men', so-called because the first example was found in South African mining deposits by Raymond Dart, the Australian Professor of Anatomy at Witwatersrand University) occupies a pivotal position as the first demonstrably upright walking direct ancestor of modern humans.

Above Donald Johnson, discoverer of the Australopithecine 'Lucy', holds the skull that marks one of archaeology's greatest finds.

Above The 'Lucy's Legacy' exhibit at Houston, Texas, raised protests in 2007 from those who argued the fossil was too fragile to transport beyond Ethiopia.

Lucy and Little Lucy

The best-known Australopithecus specimen is 'Lucy' (her scientific name is AL 288-1), the 40 per cent complete skeleton of a female of the species A. *afarensis*, who lived 3.2 million years ago in Ethiopia's Awash Valley, and whose fossil remains were found in 1974 by the International Afar Research Expedition. Lucy was 1.1m (3ft 8in) tall, weighed 29kg (65lb) and looked like an upright walking chimpanzee. Her species was the last before the human and chimpanzee lines split.

In 2000, the remains were found of another member of the same species, the near complete skeleton of a three-year-old A. *afarensis* female named Selam (Ethiopian for 'Peace'), but also known as 'Little Lucy' or 'Lucy's Baby' (although she lived 3.3 million years ago and is 120,000 years older than Lucy).

The Palaeolithic Era

*Archaeologists studying human behaviour in the Palaeolithic era, or
'Old Stone Age', look for sites where bones and tools are found together,
perhaps with evidence of fire and cooking. In fact, some researchers argue
that the study of archaeology only begins with the first evidence of tool use.*

There is an argument that the study of early hominid species, before the first evidence of tool use some 2.5 million years ago, is really a branch of palaeontology (the study of fossils), or of biology, anatomy, geology, geography or physical anthropology. It is true that many of the key figures in the field of human origins research have a background in some other discipline, but there is undoubtedly a considerable overlap between those anthropologists who study early hominid developments during the huge sweep of time spanning the last ten million years and the archaeologists who are more concerned with the last 2.5 million years – the date of the dividing line between the australopithecenes, which are, in many ways, more like primates than humans, and the first hominins, which are more like humans of today than they are like other primates. It is during this latter period that great changes in behaviour took place that mark the beginning of 'human' (instead of instinctive) thought and behaviour.

The Old Stone Age

An important marker in the development of human behaviour is the use of tools made from stone. The period when tool use develops is known as the Palaeolithic era, which is also known as the Old Stone Age. It corresponds to the geological era known as the

Above Palaeolithic axe heads are studied at an ancient site in Libya.

Pleistocene, a period of glacial episodes, or ice ages, fluctuating with warmer intervals, called interglacials. Climatic stress might have been the reason why human ancestors left the tree canopy to explore the open spaces of the savannah, why tool use developed about 2.5 million years ago and why fire was domesticated around 1.5 million years ago.

Once it was thought that only *Homo sapiens* had the conceptual capacity for tool use and fire making, but now archaeologists know that the other great apes (members of the biological

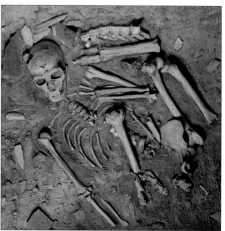

Above 45,000-year-old Neanderthal bones lie in situ at La Chapelle-aux-Saintes, France.

Left An artist's impression shows how a family of *Homo erectus* hominins might have appeared in their natural environment. This species, who were in existence 800,000 to 30,000 years ago, used stone tools and cooked with fire.

family Hominidae, which includes humans, chimpanzees, gorillas and orangutangs) also exhibit social behaviour and language use and will modify natural materials to make tools. A major difference between humans and other hominids is that the great apes are opportunistic – they will use a tool if it happens to be lying around – but do not think ahead and store or carry tools. Crucially, too, humans adapted the stones that they found to create specialist tools, some of them of great aesthetic beauty, with symmetrical profiles, rather than simply using rocks as they were found.

In fact, the current definition of what makes humans different from their primate cousins is the human's capacity to live in the world of the imagination, although, as will be seen, other hominids, all now extinct, also had this capacity. Archaeologists also now know that some of these extinct hominins, such as the Australopithecines, not only made tools but also developed lifestyles of increasing sophistication, and that some of them travelled long distances and colonized large parts of the world.

The Olduvai Gorge

In Tanzania, the Olduvai Gorge – which is known as 'The Cradle of Mankind' – occupies an iconic place in early hominid research. It is the place where so many important discoveries have been made, first by the German prehistorian Hans Reck from 1913, then by members of the Leakey family – Louis and Mary from the 1930s and their son Richard from the 1960s.

The gorge is 50km (30 miles) long and 100m (330ft) deep. Erosion by ancient rivers has revealed deep stratigraphy, with layer upon layer of ancient volcanic deposits that date back 2.5 million years. Named after this site are the very earliest tools, which are known as Oldowan, and consist of cobbles used as hammerstones and sharp-edged flakes that have been deliberately struck from a larger stone to make a variety of tools, such as scrapers, axe-shaped choppers and pointed awls.

First fire

Finding evidence of burning is not necessarily evidence that the fire was made deliberately. Archaeologists looking for the early domestication of fire look for hearth structures, areas of burning that are small and discrete (wild fires will usually scorch a large area) and for fires that are also associated with a concentration of burnt bones, stone tools, or bones that have been butchered and have cut marks or fractures.

So far the earliest generally accepted evidence of controlled fire use comes from fossil hearths and burnt animal bones from sites in Kenya and from the Swartkrans cave in South Africa, both dating from 1.5 million years ago.

Above Archaeologists search for human prehistory at the edge of Olduvai Gorge in Tanzania.

Below The elongated skull of an Australopithecene (*left*) adjacent to the more rounded skull of *Homo habilis* (*right*).

The Paleolithic era: key dates

Dates often overlap because new species and new tools co-existed alongside archaic species and tools for a period of time.

• Lower Palaeolithic (2.5 million to 120,000 years ago): Australopithecines (*Australopithecus africanus*, *A. aethipicus*, *A. garhi*, *A. boisei* and *A. robustus*) and hominins (*Homo habilis*, *H. rudolfensis* and *H. ergaster*) are all using tools, which have been found in Ethiopia, Kenya, Tanzania, Uganda and South Africa. *H. ergaster* migrates out of East Africa and adapts to a wide range of environments in Eurasia.

• Middle Palaeolithic (800,000 years ago to 30,000 years ago): Flake tools are made and used by *H. erectus*, *H. antecessor* and *H. heidelbergensis*. These are the species who populate the world as part of the first 'out of Africa' wave of migration.

• Upper Palaeolithic (100,000 years ago to 12,000 years ago): Modern humans begin the second 'out of Africa' migration and spread across the world to reach Australia and the Americas. Competition between modern humans and other hominins leads to the extinction of Neanderthals in Europe and *H. erectus* in Asia, leaving *H. sapiens* as the only surviving hominin species.

Populating the World

Although archaeologists believe that all hominin species evolved from African ancestors, their fossil remains are found all over the world, testimony to the fact that early hominins were capable of travelling long distances in search of the food that they needed for survival.

Above Footprints made in solidified lava, discovered at the Roccamonfino volcano in the Campania region of southern Italy. Archaeologists believe this is the print of the 'European' *Homo erectus*, known as *Homo heidelbergensis*, who walked this area some 300,000–325,000 years ago.

The earliest evidence of human behaviour comes from sites in Africa, but the geographical field widens once early hominins embark on what has been called 'the Great Adventure' of populating the world. In reality, it is unlikely that hominin dispersal out of Africa was the result of a decision to explore what lay beyond the horizon. Instead, archaeologists believe that rapid climate change led to the food-rich African savannah drying up about 1.9 million years ago, forcing the hominins of southern and eastern Africa to travel in search of food.

Working Man

One species in particular seems to have travelled further than the others. *Homo ergaster* ('Working Man') was given his name because of the more varied and sophisticated range of stone tools that this species made. Typically, *H. ergaster* bones and tools are found at sites in Kenya. The most spectacular find to date is the near-complete skeleton of the 'Turkana Boy', so-called because he was found on the shores of Lake Turkana, where he died around 1.5 million years ago.

H. ergaster more closely resembles modern humans than any previous hominin, with his considerably larger brain. His invention of new kinds of stone tools – hand axes, cleavers, flakes, scrapers and chopping tools – points to a new evolutionary phase, as does the wide geographical range of the sites where these tools are found. They are called Acheulian, after the first site where they were found, at Saint-Acheul in France, but they are also found right across the continent of Africa, as far east as India and as far north as southern England.

From Africa to Indonesia, China and Europe

From 1.9 million years ago, when no hominin remains or tools are found outside Africa, it is not long before we find the Acheulian-type tools associated with *H. ergaster* in use at sites in the Jordan Rift Valley, as well as in the former Soviet republic of Georgia, bordering Turkey. It has been calculated that the spread of *H. ergaster* out of Africa represents a journey of 50km (30 miles) a year – not such a big step, if that is translated into a daily average, although, of course, the landscape would have presented numerous barriers and challenges. Travelling along the coast and feeding on shellfish was probably easier than hacking a path through dense jungle, which might explain why the rainforest around the River Congo, for example, has no evidence of colonization by *H. ergaster*, whereas coastal caves and rock shelters have such evidence in relative abundance.

Those first migrants did not stop evolving. Exactly how and when is still

Above Only the discovery of more fossils will enable archaeologists to place *Homo floresiensis* within the hominin family tree.

Homo floresiensis

Scientists continue to make discoveries that suggest that other species of hominin survived until relatively recent times. The skeletal remains of *Homo floresiensis* (dubbed 'the Hobbit' by the media because of its small stature) were discovered on the Indonesian island of Flores in 2003. It was declared to be an entirely new tool-using species that had evolved from *H. erectus*, and that had survived in isolation on this island until about 18,000 years ago, making it the last hominin species other than our own to survive on the planet. However, some scientists do not accept that *H. floresiensis* is a new species. They believe the remains found on the island are those of a modern human with a neurological disorder, called microcephaly, in which the head is much smaller than average for the person's age.

a subject for research (the small amount of skeletal evidence we have for this early phase of hominid evolution would easily fit into a single laboratory) but it is thought that *H. ergaster* evolved into *H. erectus* ('Upright Man'), a species found in south-east Asia (named 'Java Man' and 'Peking Man' after their find sites) while *H. antecessor* ('Pioneer Man') appears in Europe roughly about 800,000 years ago followed by *H. heidelbergensis* ('Heidelberg Man') roughly 600,000 years ago.

Multi-regional evolution

Java Man, Peking Man, Heidelberg Man and several other hominins distinctive to a particular region of the world were once thought to be the co-equal ancestors of the different people of the world – Java Man of the south-east Asian people, Peking Man of the modern Chinese and Heidelberg Man of modern Europeans. In other words, evolutionary scientists once believed that differences in skin colour, body shape, skull shape, hair and eye type and colour could be explained as the result of the evolution of modern humans not once, but several times over, independently and in different parts of the world.

This multi-regional evolutionary theory was based on the science of morphology, which is the study of shapes and forms. Today, the study of genes

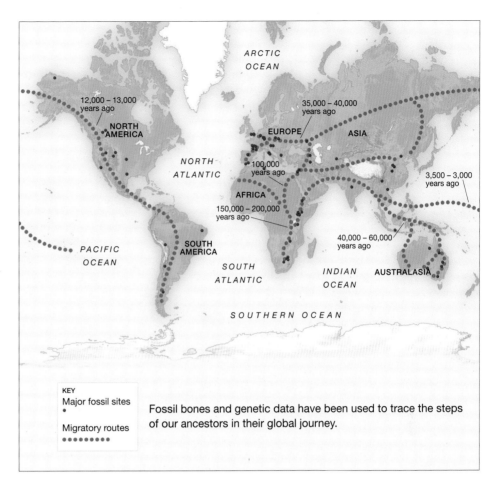

KEY
Major fossil sites
•
Migratory routes
•••••••••

Fossil bones and genetic data have been used to trace the steps of our ancestors in their global journey.

has revolutionized the classification of organic life, and the extraction of ancient DNA from fossil bones has enabled specialists in genetics to examine the degree to which modern humans are really related to these archaic species.

They have concluded that none of us is descended from Java Man, Peking Man or Heidelberg Man, and that, instead, all human beings alive today are descended from an entirely new species that evolved in Africa about 400,000 years ago – *Homo sapiens*. Although the other hominin species were very successful in colonizing their own part of the world, they are now all extinct and contributed nothing to humans' genetic inheritance. Java Man and Peking Man (*H. erectus*) continued to evolve on a different evolutionary track in Asia until becoming extinct around 60,000 years ago. In Europe, Heidelberg Man (*H. heidelbergensis*) evolved into Neanderthal Man (*H. neanderthalensis*), but neanderthals then became extinct

Above The skull of *Homo ergaster*. Note the size of the brain compared to older skulls.

Above This colour coded map, with major fossil sites marked, shows how far each species is known to have migrated on the basis of skeletal finds. *Homo erectus* travelled an extraordinary distance, reaching at least as far as the Indonesian island of Java, then part of a continuous land mass stretching from northern Europe almost to the shores of Australia.

about 23,000 years ago, leaving modern humans as the dominant hominin species.

It is possible that our species caused the extinction of these other hominins, because, like *H. ergaster*, *H. sapiens* was also a great explorer. The species began to migrate out of Africa about 100,000 years ago and, wherever it went, it encountered other hominins. It is likely that *H. sapiens* would have competed with them for food and shelter, either directly, by fighting and killing them, or indirectly, by being better hunters and depriving them of food. The latter was, in fact, becoming increasingly scarce as climate change transformed food-rich savannah into the deserts we know in Africa today.

Caves and Colonization

By carefully excavating evidence from caves and rock shelters, archaeologists have been able to track the human migrations of the Middle and Upper Paleolithic eras, which have extended from East Africa to Australia — and ultimately to the Americas.

Above Louis and Mary Leakey examine hominin remains on the shores of Lake Tanganyika.

What was it that made our *Homo sapiens* ancestors get up and leave their original home in East Africa? As with so many evolutionary developments, it seems that climate change might have been the cause. Ancient pollen evidence from sediments taken from the beds of Lakes Malawi and Tanganyika in East Africa, and from Lake Bosumtwi in Ghana, show that East Africa was subject to a prolonged drought between 100,000 and 75,000 years ago. The drought was so severe that Lake Malawi – on whose shores many early hominins lived, and now some 550km (340 miles) long and 700m (2,300ft) deep – was reduced to a couple of small lakes, no more than 10km (6 miles) across and 200m (650ft) deep. Lake Bosumtwi, currently 10km (6 miles) wide, lost all of its water.

Such a prolonged period of dry, hot weather must have had a profound impact on the landscape and on the availability of food resources. It is likely that this was what motivated some of the 10,000 or so *H. sapiens* who lived in East Africa at the time – and from whom we are all descended – to begin their global journey.

Drowned landscapes

Tracking their migrations is not easy. Early hunter-gatherers left little by way of an imprint on the earth, just as the people who live in the Amazon or in the dense rainforests of south-east Asia today leave little trace of their presence. It is probable that early migrants followed coasts and rivers – perhaps using log boats – to avoid the barriers and hazards of land-based journeys.

Left The first occupants of the Great Cave of Niah in Sarawak, Borneo, were Palaeolithic hunter-gatherers – but excavations have revealed usage up to 4,000 years ago.

Below The skull of *Australopithecus africanus* found at the Sterkfontein cave complex, South Africa, is the most complete specimen to date.

Sea levels were considerably lower than they are today because so much more of the earth's water was locked up in glaciers and the polar ice caps. Places that are now islands in southeast Asia, such as Java, Sumatra and Borneo, were once part of a continuous land mass. Much of the evidence for the earliest human journeys now lies drowned beneath the sea.

Cave archaeology

Such evidence that archaeologists do have for hominin dispersal comes from the painstaking excavation of cave sites, some of which have become famous among archaeologists: the Swartskrans, Sterkfontein and Blombos Caves (*see* The Origins of Art and Ornament) in South Africa, or the Niah Cave in Sarawak, on the island of Borneo.

Very often such cave sites were used as a natural shelter for hundreds of thousands of years, slowly building deposits. Typically, what archaeologists find is a mass of bone and stone tools, and evidence of fire. The bones found in cave deposits cannot always be assumed to be those consumed by humans. Scavengers, such as hyenas, will drag food (including humans) into caves to eat, so cave deposits often consist of a complex mix of human and animal activity.

That explains why archaeological projects at cave sites painstakingly record every find in three dimensions, aiming to reconstruct on computer the exact relationships of all the finds,

looking for patterns that might indicate a hearth, a tool manufacturing site, a butchery area, an area where skins are converted to clothing or areas where people slept, or deposited their dead, or carried out their rituals. The search for such evidence can take years and even last for a lifetime, as archaeologists continually revisit important sites to reassess the evidence or excavate new areas – often small areas, but ones that are capable of yielding enough material for years of analysis.

Migration to Australia

Mostly what is found in caves sites is very ordinary to the non-specialist. Typical of the sort of evidence that archaeologists look for when dealing with the early migration period is the Jerimalai limestone cave site on the eastern tip of the island of East Timor. This is being excavated by Sue O'Connor, Head of Archaeology and Natural History at the Australian National University, who hopes the site will answer questions about the routes taken by ancient migrants from south-east Asia to Australia – did they, as she believes, travel south, via Timor, or north, via Borneo and Sulawesi and down through Papua New Guinea?

Until now, all the habitation sites found on these 'stepping stone' islands are later in date than the earliest sites in Australia, but the Jerimalai site has yielded finds dating from 42,000 years old, and could be much older. Finds from the cave indicate that the people who sheltered here ate turtles and giant rats – but also tuna fish, which implies that boat-building and fishing skills were established at that date.

Below Jerimalai Cave in East Timor is a site that represents a missing link in the great hominid migration.

Colonizing the world

All the evidence suggests that *Homo sapiens* was on the move 100,000 years ago and migrated northward first from East Africa into North Africa and the Nile region, then eastward into south-west Asia 100,000 years ago and from there eastward into northern India, and then southward down through the Malay peninsula into Indonesia and on to Australia, which was reached 50,000 years ago. Various groups then continued the human journey westward into Europe, northward into China and Russia, eastward into Borneo and New Guinea and southward into Tasmania, all of which show signs of human presence within 40,000 years.

Above As indicated by the arrows in this world map, it is believed that *Homo sapiens* originated in eastern Africa (see nucleus), later migrating mainly to the north and east.

The Americas remained the last uncolonized continents, and there is considerable debate about the origins of their people. The genes of some southern American people suggest that they are part of a group that broke away from Australasian populations up to 35,000 years ago, suggesting that their ancestors made a hazardous ocean voyage across the Pacific to South America. This remains a controversial theory. More certain is the genetic and physical evidence that humans were present in Siberia and Japan 25,000 years ago and that the ancestors of today's Native Americans came from this part of Asia, crossing into North America in several migrations from 15,000 years ago.

The Origins of Art and Ornament

Art, in the form of sculpture, and ornament in the form of jewellery, are among the first evidence of that capacity for imagination and the use of symbols that truly distinguish humans from other forms of life. New finds keep giving earlier dates for the invention of these creative activities.

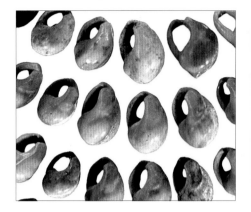

Above The Blombos Cave 'beads' are actually the pierced shells of Nassarius, or mud snails, still native to that region.

The site at Kostenki, on the banks of the River Don, 155km (250 miles) south of Moscow, has long been one of the classical sites for early human remains. However, new finds from the site indicate that it is older than first thought, dating back 47,000 years to the Upper Palaeolithic era. This makes it one of the earliest places with evidence of modern humans in Europe.

Recent finds not only include the oldest dated bone and ivory needles with eyelets yet found in Europe — probably used for tailoring animal furs to protect the settlers from the harsh climate — they also include an ivory carving that appears to show the head of a human being and marks an early attempt at figurative art. Bones from the site include hare and Arctic fox and fish, implying the use of snares and nets. Reindeer and horses were also hunted and eaten.

Large numbers of tools show that this was a well-used site. Among the tools found were a rotary drill, awls, blades, scrapers and antlers. Shells from the Black Sea – 480km (300 miles) away –

Below Neolithic rock painting of giraffes from the Tin Abaniora rock-shelter, Iherir Plateau, Tassili n'Ajjer, in Algeria *c.* 3500BC.

were used to make ornaments and most of the stone used for tool-making at the site came from 160km (100 miles) away, implying that the people who lived at Kostenki might have been trading with other groups, or that they travelled great distances to obtain raw materials.

First evidence of art

If people were carving ivory and making shell jewellery 47,000 years ago, how much further back can we

Below The 'Venus' of Dolní, Vestonice, Czech Republic, is one of the oldest representations of the human figure dating from 29,000BC.

Right The El-Wad Cave site, Mount Carmel, Israel, has been in use for 200,000 years, and includes some of the earliest human burials ever found.

push these creative activities? Every time archaeologists think they have the answer, someone makes a discovery that pushes the date further back still. In 2004, archaeologists thought the answer had been found in a string of pierced shells found in South Africa's Blombos Cave, 300km (187 miles) east of Cape Town in South Africa, on the Indian Ocean coast. The 41 Nassarius shells found date from 75,000 years ago and had been collected from a river bank (the nearest river then being 20km (12 miles) away). The shells appeared to have been selected for size and had been deliberately perforated for threading on to a string. Traces of red ochre suggest they had been coloured or were worn by someone with red ochre on their body. Two years previously, at the same cave, archaeologists found two rectangular blocks of ochre inscribed with a complex geometric pattern of rectangles and diamond shapes, dating from 77,000 years ago.

New discoveries

Then, in 2006, pierced shells from two separate sites were found whose dating pushes back the date for bead-working to at least 100,000 years ago. The shells were excavated between 1931 and 1932 from the Middle Palaeolithic site at Es-Skhul, Mount Carmel, Israel, and from Oued Djebbana, Bir-el-Ater, Algeria. The original excavators had concentrated on human remains and tools, so the significance of the shells had not been appreciated at the time. Microscopic analysis shows that the shells had been artificially pierced, probably with flint tools, and may have been hung on sinew, fibres or leather for use as pendants or in necklaces.

As for body art, archaeologists now have evidence that rock tools from the Twin Rivers hilltop cave near Lusaka in Zambia were used for grinding pigments 300,000 years ago – before

Homo sapiens even began their migrations – and not just the red of ochre, but a whole repertoire of colours that include yellow, brown, black and purple.

So archaeologists know that people in Africa were capable of the kinds of thinking that lead to the deliberate creation of patterns and jewellery and the use of minerals for body ornament as far back as the Middle Palaeolithic era. No doubt future finds will push the date for artistic and ornamental behaviour back further still, along with the origins of the key survival skills – boat-building, fishing, clothes-making, hunting and trade – implied by finds from Australia and Russia.

Left This reconstruction shows how three holes pierced at regular intervals might have converted the hollow femur bone of a bear into the world's earliest known flute. The remains of the third hole can be seen on the left.

Creative Neanderthals

What should not be forgotten is that *Homo sapiens* were not the only hominins capable of complex thought, religious belief and artistic creativity. There is a growing body of evidence to show that *Homo heidelbergensis* used ochre as body decoration and that Neanderthals buried their dead in graves, along with offerings of pierced shell jewellery.

Neanderthals might even have developed musical instruments. What is claimed to be the world's oldest flute was found in 1995 in the Divje Babe I cave in western Slovenia. Found in 43,000-year-old Neanderthal occupation layers, it consists of the femur (upper leg bone) of a cave bear punctuated by three holes. It is almost impossible to say whether this really is a musical instrument or, as some academics believe, whether the holes were made by a carnivorous animal simply chewing on the bone.

The Mesolithic Period

Also referred to as the Middle Stone Age, the Mesolithic period is an archaeological period that bridges the Old (Palaeolithic) and New (Neolithic) Stone Ages. It is a period in which the pace of technological development speeds up.

During the Mesolithic period, the 'toolkit' becomes more varied and specialist in function and humans begin to have a bigger impact on the landscape, with the first evidence of tree clearance and monument building. The Mesolithic period is also one in which the climate plays an important part in human development. It is an archaeological period that equates to the Holocene in geology – that is, the period during which the repeated glaciations of the previous era (the Palaeolithic in archaeology, the Pleistocene in geology) begin to give way to longer periods of warm weather – interglacials – during which the glaciers melt and sea levels rise.

With the Mesolithic period, archaeologists have reached the point in human

Below This ancient Mesopotamian relief depicts the mytical flood saga of Gilgamesh.

history where it is no longer possible to talk about changes that take place simultaneously and on a global scale – from now on, archaeology is increasingly varied and regional, with different people living at different levels of development. Early humans living in sites furthest from the Equator had to overcome greater challenges to survive. By contrast, people in Africa, Asia and Australia were far less affected by glacial cold, and the transitional period from the nomadic hunter-gatherer lifestyle of the Palaeolithic period to the settled agricultural life of the Neolithic period is faster and earlier than the same transition in Europe. In south-west Asia, the period between the Old and New Stone Ages is so brief that it is called the Epipaleolithic (meaning 'beyond' the Old Stone Age) rather than the Mesolithic, or Middle Stone Age.

Above The rising water levels of interglacial periods meant that land masses, and with them entire communities, were suddenly lost.

A different world

What also adds to the growing complexity of this period is the way that the map of the world was redrawn as the ice melted. This was not a single smooth event, but instead consisted of a series of cold and warmer periods, during which the glaciers retreated and advanced several times, although each time the cold snaps were less severe than the last.

As the ice melted, the world began to change in ways that created the more familiar geography of today. Instead of a slow rise in the average sea level, there were various tipping points when sudden flooding drowned very large areas of land. In fact, this was how the Mediterranean Sea was created, and

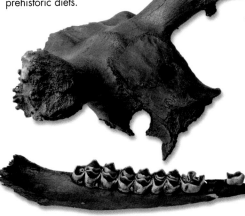

Below Remains found at Star Carr, northern England, including a frontlet (*top*) and the jawbone (*bottom*) of a red deer, tell us something of prehistoric diets.

how the islands of Indonesia, Malaysia, Papua New Guinea and Japan were separated from the mainland and from each other. Tasmania became separated from Australia and the British Isles were cut off from the European continent when water poured into the marshy plains south and east of England, thereby creating the North Sea and English Channel.

The distant mythologized memory of such cataclysmic events is recorded in the Bible, as are the many other traumas of the past – including drought, plague, famine, sickness and plagues of locusts – that early human society suffered as a consequence. There is another echo of these difficult times in the flood story in the ancient Mesopotamian Epic of Gilgamesh, which was written down in the third millennium BC.

Ritual and religion

The Mesolithic period is thus a time in which people had to respond to change and uncertainty, as the landscape in which they lived was transformed, sometimes with astonishing and violent rapidity. Perhaps it is no surprise that this is a period in which archaeologists find increasing amounts of evidence for ritualistic or religious practice and for a growing sense of social organization – which could be interpreted as a banding together to form a common front against an uncertain world.

Archaeologists have many examples of the burial of individuals in isolated graves from the Palaeolithic period, but the Mesolithic period sees the first cemeteries – communal burial places that are used over several generations – in Russia and Ukraine. The grave goods from Oleneostrovski Mogilnik, in Russia, include carved figures – material evidence for the growing importance of the symbolic and spiritual dimensions to life.

People were beginning at this time not just to live in the landscape, but also to modify it for their own use – and not just for economic reasons. As recently as 2007, 12 massive post pits at Warren Field in Crathes, south-west of Aberdeen, in Scotland, have been radiocarbon dated to the Mesolithic period (8000–7500BC). This dating proves that Mesolithic people built big monuments – the size of the pits implies a row of massive tree-trunk sized columns – and challenges the idea that monument building is a later Neolithic innovation. Three similarly massive post holes dating from 8000BC are the earliest evidence of monument making, and these are at the site of Stonehenge in southern England.

Mesolithic ritual seems to have included feasting. Excavating the site of Heathrow Terminal 5, in southern England, archaeologists have found large pits filled with burnt bone and stones that were interpreted as evidence of ritual feasting. The quantity of stones suggests that the site was used for this purpose over many years. And at Star Carr, a Mesolithic site buried beneath a bog in Yorkshire, England – once a lake-edge settlement – excavators found red deer skulls and antlers that had been pierced to be worn as headdresses – nobody is sure whether the antlers were worn by hunters as a disguise, or as some sort of religious or ceremonial costume.

Right The skeleton of an 18-year-old male who was buried with a shell hat and necklace at the Mesolithic site of Arene Candide in Italy.

Above One of the flints found at Pakefield in eastern England.

The settlement of the British Isles

Humans tried to colonize Britain seven times over a 700,000-year period before the ancestors of today's population put down roots some 12,000 years ago. From 32 flint tools found in sediments exposed by erosion at the bottom of a cliff in Pakefield, near the Suffolk seaside town of Lowestoft, archaeologists know that there were tool-using hominins in East Anglia 700,000 years ago, but there were also long periods – of 100,000 years in duration – when the climate was too cold for anyone to live in northern Europe.

Drowned Landscapes

Because so much of the evidence for the Mesolithic period lies beneath the sea, finding it presents all kinds of challenges. Archaeologists have responded by borrowing techniques from seismology, by digging bogs and by wading in coastal mud.

Above Archaeologists are rising to the challenge of reconstructing historic landscapes now hidden beneath sea or salt marsh.

The drowned landscapes that hold so much information about our past are not entirely lost forever. For example, cod fishing fleets working the Dogger Bank in the North Sea have been trawling up worked flints, antler tools, and the bones of reindeer, mammoth and woolly rhino for centuries. Yet, only now has the marshy land mass – 22,000km sq (8,500 miles sq) in extent – that once connected the present east coast of England with northern Germany, Denmark and Norway been explored in more detail.

A hidden landscape

Geological surveying in the North Sea in the search for oil has produced a mass of seismic evidence that archaeologists at Birmingham University have turned into a map of Doggerland, an entire European country that has not been seen for 8,500 years or more. So detailed is the seismic data that the archaeologists have been able to reconstruct the rivers, streams, lakes and coastlines of a uniquely preserved Mesolithic landscape covering an area the size of Wales.

The results of this North Sea Palaeolandscapes project ('palaeo' here does not relate to the period – it is used as the term for 'old') have excited archaeologists in all the countries that bound the North Sea basin. Their next big challenge is to look for likely areas of Mesolithic settlement and come up with ways of exploring these underwater sites. Two such sites have already begun to be excavated. One lies 11m (36ft) beneath the sea off the Isle of Wight's Bouldnor Cliff. Divers have already found hundreds of worked flints, charred stones from two hearths and a possible log canoe. The other is in Denmark, where the construction of a major road and rail bridge in the Storebælt region led to the excavation of a wealth of new archaeological evidence for this period, including one of the defining characteristics of Mesolithic sites, the 'composite' tool, so-called because it is made of more than one material – for example, a flint blade inserted into a bone handle, a spearhead set into a wooden shaft, or a series of small flints (called 'microliths' or 'microblades') set into a shaft for use as barbed harpoons or arrows.

Seabed prehistory

Another technique archaeologists use to probe beneath the sea is to push tubes known as Vibrocores deep into the seabed. The tubes capture columns of sediment, including layers of ancient soil that can be analysed for evidence of human activity. The sediment can also be correlated with geological evidence to reconstruct the terrain, and it can be analysed for trapped seeds, pollen and mollusc shells to recreate ancient environments and habitats before the sea drowned the landscape.

The results of one such investigation have been used to recreate the Mesolithic landscape of the Arun Estuary in West Sussex (*see opposite page*). You can see the animated results by visiting Wessex Archaeology: www.wessexarch.co.uk/projects/marine/alsf/seabed_prehistory/computer models.html.

Left This seismic map of Doggerland shows the Mesolithic coastline along with river valleys ('fluvial systems') which would have attracted animals and their hunters.

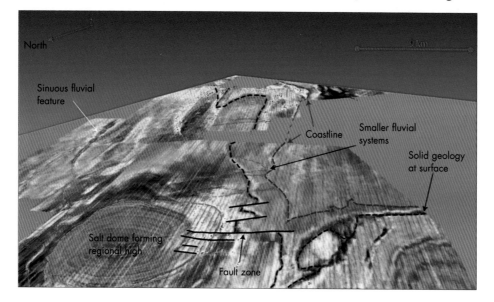

North

Sinuous fluvial feature

Coastline

Smaller fluvial systems

Solid geology at surface

Salt dome forming regional high

Fault zone

Left At the end of the last ice age, the River Arun, Sussex, UK, flowed a further 13km (8 miles) out into the English Channel than it does today. To fully recreate the valley settlement, Wessex Archaeology created models of human activity and of the likely vegetation.

Intertidal archaeology

Rising sea levels caused by melting glaciers have drowned some low-lying landscapes, which is an obvious effect. However, there is an unexpected effect of the melting glaciers that is not so obvious: some landscapes actually rose upward as the weight and pressure of the ice cap was removed. For example, the ancient shorelines in Scotland, Scandinavia and Canada are now some 8m (26ft) higher than the current average sea level, and that is why the skeletons of sea mammals are sometimes found at sites that are well above, rather then below, the present-day waterline.

Today, the sea levels are rising again, scouring soft and vulnerable coastlines and inland estuaries. This action is revealing long-buried ancient sites at a rate that worries many archaeologists who lack the resources to record all the material that is being revealed before it is destroyed by the rising sea levels.

Ancient bogs

Sometimes evidence is found on land that has become waterlogged. At the Star Carr early Mesolithic site in Yorkshire, England, first excavated by Grahame Clark in the 1950s, the waterlogged conditions of the peat bog covering the site had preserved the wood, bone and antlers that had been used to make arrows and knifes,

mattocks and chisels around 8770BC. Other finds included birch bark, used in tanning animal hides, a wooden platform made of split poplar planks, and even a wooden paddle, used to propel a boat or canoe.

Clark's analysis of the site had far-reaching implications. He found charcoal from burnt reed and birch as evidence for the deliberate clearance of the lakeside site not once but repeatedly over a period of years, which he interpreted as seasonal occupation and use of the site for hunting the deer, elk, pig and aurochs

(primitive cattle) and wildfowl whose bones were also found at the site. This is evidence that some groups of people were already tending toward the more settled way of life that defines the Neolithic period: of deliberate exploitation of the landscape on a planned basis; of organized craft and industry; and of social organization over and above that of the immediate family members.

Star Carr can be paralleled by other sites representing other cultures in transition. Dating from 18,000BC is a similar site that was found in Israel in 1989 when the waters of the Sea of Galilee fell to a very low level, thereby revealing the submerged remains of wooden huts made of oak, and a wealth of animal bone and plant remains. However, what made this site Epipaleolithic rather than Neolithic was the discovery that the food remains found there – including wheat, barley and beans – were still being gathered from wild plants, rather than being from domesticated varieties.

Right This mesolithic blade, measuring 100mm (4in) long, was an effective tool for butchery and food preparation.

Footprints in the mud

Intertidal archaeology involves the strenuous work of monitoring shorelines and estuary margins for the evidence of human activity. The work is demanding because it often involves wading through thick mud in all weathers to record evidence that is only revealed for a short period of time before being covered up again. Some of the evidence is only revealed for a few days before being eroded away by scouring tides.

The result can be the most intimate of encounters with our human ancestors. For example, one site on the River Severn estuary at Goldcliff, near Newport, Gwent, south Wales, has revealed the footprints of children playing on a river bank one sunny day in the Mesolithic period. Mixed in with the children's footprints were those of cranes, aurochs and the deer that their parents were no doubt hunting when they were not fishing for eels.

The Neolithic Period

The era in which people began to grow crops and keep animals is known as the Neolithic, or New Stone Age, period. It led to a huge shift in lifestyles, from a nomadic, opportunistic existence based on hunting and gathering wild food to land clearance and semi-permanent settlements.

In areas of the world less affected by ice age glaciations something new and revolutionary was beginning to happen. Blessed with a climate that encourages rich biodiversity – including animals, such as horses, and plants, such as apples, that were unknown to the Mesolithic hunter-gatherers in northern Europe – the people of south-west Asia began to select and domesticate some animal species, to cultivate certain types of seed and plant, and to lead more settled lives, clearing the landscape of its wild vegetation, living in villages, herding animals, tilling and irrigating fields.

As with so many innovations, such activities are not exclusive to the Neolithic period and can be traced back to a much earlier era. Dogs were first domesticated as hunting partners perhaps 35,000 years ago, and they are found buried with humans in pre-agricultural cemeteries in many parts of the world, from Mesolithic Skateholm in Sweden to the Koster site in Illinois. The careful management of food sources probably dates back thousands of years. The indigenous people of Australia, for example, while living a hunter-gatherer lifestyle, always return part of the plant tubers they dig up to the ground. The earliest known oven and the earliest evidence of grain milling come from a site called Ohalo II, situated on the south-western shore of the Sea of Galilee and date back 15,000 years, around 4,000 years before either wheat or barley were domesticated.

Above Cultivated crops brought about a revolution in human behaviour.

However, the Neolithic period sees an intensification of such behaviour, and an acceleration of the range of animals and crops that are managed. In addition, it is called the Neolithic – the New Stone Age – because of the innovative stone tools that become more common at this time, such as sickles and grindstones specifically connected with agriculture and cereal use.

The Fertile Crescent

The credit for the development of agriculture is traditionally given to the Fertile Crescent region of the Middle East. The term was coined by James Henry Breasted (1865–1935), the first

Above Excavating a dog at the Neolithic site of Ashqelon, Israel. Although the domestication of these animals gained momentum in the Neolithic, the origins of the practice are much earlier.

Above The huge city of Tel Hazor in Galilee began life as a prehistoric farming community.

Right The well-preserved floor of a 'brush hut', where food preparation would have taken place, excavated at the Neolithic site Ohalo II, Israel (*right*), and a gazelle horn core (*far right*), discovered close to a hearth at the site. An artist's reconstruction of a Neolithic brush hut (*below right*).

Above Two of the figs discovered at the Gilgal I site in Jordan.

Founder crops

Nine small figs recently discovered in a house in the early Neolithic village called Gilgal I, in the Jordan Valley, might be the earliest evidence yet of agriculture. The carbonized fruits come from a variety of fig that produces large but sterile fruits. Such mutations occur in the wild, but since they produce no seed, the plant will eventually die without offspring – they can only survive if a human being recognizes the value of the larger fruits and deliberately removes shoots or roots and plants them. Radiocarbon dating dated these figs to 11,400 years ago, and they are the earliest evidence so far of the consumption of a domestic crop, rather than a wild plant.

Figs are one of the so-called 'founder crops' that grow wild in the Fertile Crescent. The others include emmer wheat, einkorn, barley, flax, chickpea, pea, lentil and bitter vetch (a plant with lentil-like seeds). All are relatively easy to grow and it is possible that wild seed was gathered and sown in cultivated fields long before people had the idea of selective breeding.

American to earn a university doctorate in the study of ancient Egypt and the first Professor of Egyptology and Oriental History in the United States (appointed in 1905 by the University of Chicago). He used the term to describe a region that includes the Nile, Jordan, Euphrates and Tigris Rivers and stretches from the eastern shores of the Mediterranean to the Persian Gulf, taking in present-day Egypt, Israel, the West Bank, the Gaza Strip, Lebanon, parts of Jordan, Syria and Iraq and south-eastern Turkey and south-western Iran. Breasted recognized the natural fertility of the region's soils and their seasonal irrigation by region's rivers. He and other archaeologists noted that this was the home of some of the earliest complex societies. It is commonly known, from its shape on the map, as 'The Fertile Crescent'.

Multiple origins

However, this classic view of the Fertile Crescent as the source of all that we associate with the Neolithic revolution has since been challenged, as archaeologists in other parts of the world have found evidence that domesticated crops were developed by different people in geographically distant places.

If each domesticated animal or food plant derived from a single point of origin (as humans do), each species would have a homogeneous gene profile. In fact, ancient crops show distinct regional variations. Grains from Neolithic deposits in the Fertile Crescent have been compared to barley of the similar age from 3,000km (1,875 miles) further east in Central Asia. In every case there was close match between the domesticated barley and its local wild version, and

far less of a match between the two domesticated strains. This means that the farmed varieties were developed independently, many times over.

Similarly, archaeologists have found evidence for the invention of farming in parts of the world with no possibility of contact with people who already had the skill. When Europeans reached the New World, for example, they found steep hillsides carved into terraces where people cultivated potato, tomato, pepper, squash, several varieties of bean, maize, manioc and tobacco, and recent research has suggested that some of these crops were first domesticated in the Americas around 5200BC.

Finds from China give a date of around 7500BC for the earliest example of domesticated rice yet found, though it was not until 5000BC that domesticated rice strains are the dominant form of food consumed. As new finds are made, the traditional view that rice was domesticated in China's Yangtze Delta and spread from there is being challenged by evidence of early rice cultivation in Korea, Japan and northern India, while an entirely different strain of rice was first cultivated in the Sahel region of Africa, along with the sorghum, one of the staple grains of the modern African diet, before 5000BC.

The Spread of Agriculture

Gordon Childe, the Australian archaeologist who was one of the first to try to understand the origins and spread of agriculture, coined the phrase 'Neolithic Revolution' to imply that this was a sudden and all-changing phenomenon. Archaeologists now know that the picture is more complex.

Above Wild wheat growing in the Near East. It was first cultivated 11,000 years ago.

Not only is the development of agriculture far more complex than the idea of a single invention, it also seems to have been a protracted process. Wheat spikelets from Neolithic settlements in northern Syria and south-eastern Turkey have recently been analysed to compare the ratio of wild to domesticated wheat at various dates. At the 10,500-year-old site called Nevali Çori in Turkey, 90 per cent of the spikelets were from wild varieties, while 64 per cent were still wild at the 8,500-year-old site at el Kerkh in Syria and only 36 per cent were wild at 7,500-year-old Kosak Shamali, also in Syria.

This suggests that the cultivation of wild plants began 10,000 to 12,000 years ago, when farmers began saving the seed from selected plants with desirable characteristics and planting them as cultivated crops, but that they also continued to harvest wild wheat, and to consume both in their diet. There was no sudden replacement of wild varieties with selected ones – in fact, it was another 3,000 years before domesticated varieties began to be the dominant choice.

How did it spread?

Similarly, long periods of time separate the development of farming in south-west Asia and its spread to the distant reaches of Europe. Pinning down exactly how long it took has also shed light on how farming practices were spread. One hypothesis is that successful farmers moved out from south-west Asia in search of new land, colonizing new territory at the expense of indigenous hunter-gatherer communities. Another entirely different hypothesis proposes that successful ideas spread rapidly, therefore, farming techniques were adopted by indigenous hunter-gatherer communities once they could see the clear advantages that it brought to their farming neighbours.

If agriculture was spread by the movement of people, archaeologists would expect to find clear evidence of this in the DNA record. They could look for the evidence of Asian genes in the European population, representing the legacy of people whose successful strategies for survival enabled them to migrate and colonize new territories.

Recent studies have indeed found that south-west Asian genes account for about 12 per cent of Europe's population. However, it found that most of the people with such genes live within a 1,000-km (625-mile) radius of the Fertile Crescent (*see The Iron Age*). The number drops by half at 2,000km (1,250 miles) and is negligible by 3,000km (1,875 miles). In other words, it is entirely possible that small pioneer groups could have carried farming into those areas of Europe closest to the Middle East – and we can pinpoint places, such as Crete, that we know to have been directly colonized

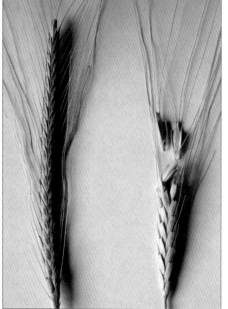

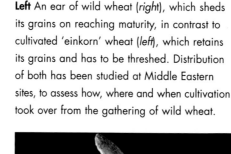

Left An ear of wild wheat (*right*), which sheds its grains on reaching maturity, in contrast to cultivated 'einkorn' wheat (*left*), which retains its grains and has to be threshed. Distribution of both has been studied at Middle Eastern sites, to assess how, where and when cultivation took over from the gathering of wild wheat.

Left The remains of charred wheat at Neolithic farming sites in the Middle East have supplied a wealth of material for studying and carbon dating ancient agricultural produce.

Above Each of the Neolithic houses at Skara Brae, on Orkney, Scotland, has a large square central hearth for heating and cooking.

Above Poulnabrone Dolmen, the Burren, Ireland; such monuments act as statements of ancestral land ownership.

Monuments and land ownership

The rise of farming is associated with the building of majestic monuments, many of them so well constructed that they have survived several millennia to be designated as World Heritage Sites, including the impressive chamber tombs of Ireland and Spain, the remarkable stone rows and megalithic structures of Brittany and the large Neolithic settlement at Skara Brae on the west coast of mainland Orkney, Scotland, which Gordon Childe excavated in between 1928 and 1930.

One explanation for the simultaneous rise of farming and monument building is the need to stamp your claim to ownership on the landscape. Once people stop regarding the whole of the landscape as a resource for all, once they begin to clear the wilderness and create fields, once they begin to invest time and effort in the building of houses, an important threshold has been crossed – one begins to develop proprietorial feelings based in the investment of labour and the resources used in creating that fertile landscape.

For all these and many other reasons, archaeologists can speculate that the consolidation of farming as a way of life led to the construction of new forms of communal structure that are used for burial, ritual and for the reinforcement of kinship ties through feasting and betrothals – and for making a visible public statement about the community's entitlement to the land.

in this way because the plants and animals and even the female figurines are the same as those in Neolithic Turkey. However, the uptake of agriculture deeper into northern and western Europe has to be the result of people copying their neighbours and learning from them – the so-called diffusion model for the spread of innovative ideas, instead of the displacement model based on the mass movement of people.

A slow journey

Attempts to trace the path and chronology of agriculture by carbon dating suggests that agriculture arrived in Europe by two routes – via the Balkans and via the Mediterranean – and that it spread across Europe in fits and starts, in a long, slow process that took several thousand years. For a long time, agriculture spread no further than the Carpathian Plain in Hungary.

This so-called halt on the onward journey of farming has been explained by biologists as a period during which cereals from Asia had to undergo further selection to find strains better adapted to the colder, wetter environments of Europe. Some archaeologists argue that the hunter-gatherer communities had to become domesticated – in other words, to overcome their resistance to farming, and to adopt the settled lifestyles that go with it.

Left Crop threshing techniques still used by pre-industrial societies help archaeobotanists to understand how prehistoric peoples processed their crops. This Nepalese community continues to rely upon this ancient agricultural method.

Metallurgy

In the three-age system, the Neolithic period gives way to the Bronze Age, but this is a term that needs some explanation, because the Copper Age comes before the Bronze Age in some parts of the world and in other parts the Iron Age follows the Stone Age with no copper or bronze phases.

Above The Trundholm sun chariot (1400BC): a spectacular example of Bronze-Age technology.

Like agriculture, metallurgy seems to have been discovered independently in many different regions. Archaeologists have found copper tools dating from 4800BC at Mehrgarh, in Baluchistan,

Pakistan, a site that has also produced some of the earliest evidence of farming (7000BC) in the Middle East. Of similar date is Wadi Faynan, in Jordan, where slag and ore has been found close to a known source of copper, and in the Timna Valley in Israel, currently held to be the oldest known copper mine in the world. In addition, raw unprocessed copper was also beaten into tools and weapons as early as 4000BC at the Old Copper Complex, in present-day Michigan and Wisconsin in the United States.

Left Ancient Egyptian copper mining at Timna Park, in modern Israel, left these formations named 'King Solomon's Pillars'.

The earliest appearance of true bronze (a stronger metal than copper, which is made by adding tin and arsenic to the copper ore) occurs in sites in Iran in the late 4th and the beginning of the 3rd millennium BC. By the mid-3rd millennium BC the skill of making bronze has been acquired by people living in a large area extending from the Persian Gulf to the Aegean.

The transition from stone to copper, and from copper to bronze, was not a one-way street – it did not lead to the immediate replacement of obsolescent stone tools with modern shiny metal. On the contrary, early metal objects deliberately copy their stone and wooden antecedents, while stone battle-axes are found in the graves of the northern European Corded Ware culture of 3,200BC onward that are modelled on copper axes, with lines carved to imitate the appearance of the mould marks on cast metal axes.

The magic of metal

The earliest use of metal consists of jewellery made from gold and copper – visible metallic elements that can be mined relatively easily. Many of the objects that define the earliest of the metal-using civilizations seem to be designed for ornamental use, as gifts for the gods and for use in ceremonies, rather than as work tools or weapons.

Left This roundhouse at Flag Fen, near the town of Peterborough, UK, reconstructs the appearance of a typical Bronze-Age dwelling.

Above This Bronze-Age stone circle on Machrie Moor, Isle of Arran, Scotland, replaced an earlier Neolithic timber circle.

In 18th and 19th century Europe, some of the most spectacular finds from the Bronze Age were dug or ploughed up by farmers and peat cutters, and today early metalwork is often found by metal detectorists, especially in watery landscapes that have since dried up, or on river foreshores such as the Thames in London, England. Rivers and lakes seem to have been favoured places for objects to be deposited as gifts to the gods – and not just any old gifts – some of the finds from peat bogs and fens include objects of the highest craftsmanship, unique pieces that would have needed skill and patience to create, such as the astonishing sun chariot of Trundholm, in Denmark, a bronze statue of a horse pulling the sun across the sky in a chariot, deposited in a bog sometime in the 15th century BC. It is as if there is a belief that metal, obtained by the transforming power of fire on rock, is regarded as something mystical and god-given, a gift that demands in return something back from its human beneficiaries.

Landscape clearance

In time, however, the development of more utilitarian metalwork led to a speeding up of the process by which the wilderness was tamed. Environmental archaeologists now believe that the Bronze Age (from about 3500BC) was the period in which the process of landscape clearance, which began in the Neolithic period, finally sped up. The Bronze Age is when there was a transformation of large tracts of woodland – interspersed with occasional clearings – into a settled landscape consisting of farms and the occasional woods, as well as fields, hedges, tracks, cattle enclosures, ponds and water scapes and drove roads.

Below The caves at Qumran result from early mining and were later used as a hiding place for the jars containing the Dead Sea Scrolls.

The trees that were cut down to create fields were not wasted, but were used for constructing houses and trackways – some of which provide access into the watery landscapes of fen and lakes, where wildfowl and fish can be trapped. The huge effort involved in taming and farming the landscape is based on the availability of sharp-edged lightweight and portable metal tools in the form of axes, adzes and chisels, and the evidence for this comes from dateable timbers found preserved in waterlogged sites, where the size and shape of the cut marks used to shape the timbers for causeways and house platforms exactly match the axes found at the site.

Above Nordic Bronze-Age petroglyphs depicting a ship on the Vitlyckehäll stone near Tanumshede, in western Sweden.

Specialization

The significance of metallurgy does not lie only in the availability of new technologies, new weapons, and new forms of defence (shields and armour), nor in finely wrought luxury goods, such as jewellery, ritual bowls, cauldrons, bells and incense burners. Just as importantly, it is in this period that some archaeologists believe there is a rise of specialist functions – in which some people make their living from their craft, as metalworkers, potters or farmers – in which trade plays a part, and in which there is the opportunity for accumulating wealth through the exercise of a particular skill, through trade or the monopolistic control of the resources for making metal.

The Iron Age

The last of the three traditional divisions of Old World prehistory is the Iron Age (from 1200BC). It stretches back to the first farmers and continues to the classical cultures of Greece and Rome in Europe and the complex societies of Africa, Asia and the Americas.

One of the insights that archaeologists are beginning to develop through the study of whole landscapes rather than isolated sites is the degree of continuity that can mark the long sweep of pre-history. This is evident in the way that succeeding generations respect the monuments of the past when they build new monuments.

Stonehenge in the south of England, for example, has been built and rebuilt many times. Although the circle of giant trilithons – the sets of three stones consisting of two uprights joined by a horizontal lintel – that defines the most popular image of Stonehenge dates from the Neolithic of 2500BC, there are earlier structures and circles on the site dating back to the first Mesolithic post holes of

around 8000BC. In addition, the circle itself is surrounded by hundreds of Bronze- and Iron-Age burial mounds.

Another example of this innate conservatism and respect for tradition is the slow rate at which iron was adopted as a material for tools and weapons. There is evidence to show that iron-making was practised in the Middle Bronze Age. Simple iron tools are known in the Netherlands by soon after 1300BC, and evidence for early iron-making in Britain, at the Bronze Age village of Hartshill Quarry in Berkshire, England, has recently been dated to 1260BC. Ironically, the earliest iron tools in Europe are punches and engraving tools that were probably used for cutting decoration onto the surface of bronze objects.

Above Reconstructions of Iron-Age roundhouses of wood and reed suggest they were surprisingly comfortable.

Trade and inflation

Perhaps what caused the switch from bronze to iron as the predominant metal was some sort of disruption to the trade routes through which tin – an essential material for making bronze – was obtained and distributed from various mines as far apart as Cornwall, Brittany, Galicia and the Italian island of Elba. Evidence for disruption, or an escalation in the price of such materials, can be found in the large numbers of hoards of broken bronze objects that are found in late Bronze Age contexts, probably saved for recycling.

Many more societies had access to supplies of the relatively abundant iron ore than had access to tin. Bronze continued to be used for coinage, brooches, jewellery, military equipment,

Below The loops on these Iron-Age axes from Spain were used to tie the axe head to a wooden shaft.

Below The Castro de Barona Iron-Age hillfort, the home of an Iberian Celtic clan, sits on a peninsula jutting out into the sea.

bells and horse harnesses for another 2,000 years but the cheaper, stronger and more abundant iron became the metal of choice for tools and weaponry. Robust iron ploughs and spades enabled heavier soils to be cultivated, and something as humble and ordinary as the iron nail made it easier to construct durable buildings.

Warfare and control

It has been argued that the greater availability of iron also led to the rise of warfare during this period, because those cultures that possessed iron-making skills were able to equip larger armies. Equally, it could be argued that the equipping of armies was not the cause of war, but rather the symptom of an age of increasing conflict, perhaps related to population growth and competition for resources.

The Roman answer to competition was conquest. From small beginnings as a small Iron-Age settlement on the River Tiber, the Romans began by conquering their neighbours, including the Etruscans, descendants of metal-working migrants who had settled in Italy to exploit the rich ores there, and then went on to carve out a massive empire taking in much of modern Europe and western Asia.

Above Ancient weaponry is reconstructed and used as part of an investigation into the lives of Iron-Age people living in Denmark.

The Iron Age continued well into the post-Roman period in parts of Europe that lay outside the Roman Empire, and it is in many ways more enigmatic to archaeologists than the more distant past. In their desire to explain, arch-aeologists often simplify and overlook facts that do not fit their story. For a long time, accounts of the Iron Age have portrayed this as a period of growing homogenization – that is, the beginning of a process that we now call globalization, when we all became more alike in our lifestyles.

Now, archaeologists are looking at the Iron Age again and finding evidence of the contrary – a period of diversity and experimentation, some of which is backward looking (ancient religious sites were reused in the Iron Age after

being abandoned for up to 1,000 years) and some of which is progressive – for example, literary and archaeological sources show that the Romans prized and imported geese, soap, amber, hides and clothing and wagons manufactured by the Iron-Age people of Germany.

Below A refuge and a fishing base: the Araisi Lake fortress at Gauja, Latvia.

Above This La Tène pot discovered at a burial mound in Brittany, northern France, has typical geometric patterning, and would have been used as a cremation urn.

Who were the Celts?

The dominant Iron-Age culture of Europe found north of the Alps is often called Celtic, a culture that is instantly linked with the curvilinear patterning that decorates metalwork items, such as mirrors and shields (such as the Battersea shield, found in the River Thames at Battersea, London, and now in the British Museum), and other objects.

The idea that the people of northern Europe were all Celts seems to have arisen from confusion among 18th- and 19th-century linguistic scholars who noted the overlap between Celtic art and its survival into the Dark-Age Gaelic speaking parts of Atlantic Europe. They hypothesized the Celtic decorative style and the so-called Celtic languages were part of the same cultural package – Celtic speakers produced Celtic art – which, in turn, was used to suggest that the Celts were a people who migrated and spread from some point of origin in Europe, who spread to dominate northern Europe but then were pushed to the margins of western Europe by the Romans.

Now archaeologists believe that so-called Celtic art (also known as La Tène art) originated in the Rhineland, the border region between the Germanic east and the Gallic west of Europe, and that it spread because it was fashionable among the different native people of Europe, rather than through the migration of people. As for the Celtic languages, they were perhaps only spoken by the people of the Atlantic west, restricted to the inhabitants of west Gaul, western Iberia, Ireland, Wales, Scotland and the west of England. In other words, there was no Celtic migration, no Celtic race that once dominated Europe; instead Celticity is all about those phenomena of markets, fashion and consumption.

Complex Societies

The more archaeologists have learnt about the past, the more obvious it has become that human cultures are far more complex than can be conveyed by the three-age system and the use of such simple terms as stone, copper, bronze and iron to describe a specific age, or era, in our past.

The three-age system is based on the observation that simple technologies tell archaeologists something about our ancestor's lifestyles and interactions. Their toolkits are a good indication of their core activities and capabilities, and when these same toolkits are found in association with dwellings of a particular size and shape or pottery of a specific design, it is not unreasonable to deduce that this represents a related group of people, even if they are spread out over a vast geographic terrain.

However, to characterize our own age as simply the 'Silicon Age' would tell archaeologists of the future nothing about the rich lives that people often lead today. Likewise, the terms applied in a similar way to past eras, such as the Stone Age, tell archaeologists little about the many differences that exist between the Bronze Ages in various region, such as China, the Aegean, Ireland, Pakistan or Wisconsin.

Subdivisions

Today, there is an increasing tendency for archaeologists to distinguish these regional subcategories and qualify their use of the three-age system by writing about the Aegean Bronze Age, the Atlantic Bronze Age or the Andean Bronze Age. These regional categories are then further subdivided into periods – for example, Early, Middle and Late Bronze Age. Archaeologists can distinguish further subcultures on the basis of tool shape or pottery variations – hence the distinction in the Neolithic of western Europe between 'Beaker' culture (pottery with a distinctive inverted bell-shaped profile)

and the Corded Ware culture (pottery decorated by pressing woven cord into the semi-dry pottery before firing).

However, for some archaeologists, even these distinctions are too broad and blunt. They reject the notion that cultures can be classified in such simplistic terms and prefer to highlight the unique characteristics of individual sites. There is some validity to this approach. Stonehenge is genuinely unique in that no other henge in the world has trilithons. Conversely, henges, as a monument type, are found all over Neolithic Europe, so many archaeologists accept that the sites they study have characteristics that are unique but also that enable them to be compared and classified.

Above Pottery excavated at Delos, the mythical birthplace of Apollo, Greek god of light, medicine and music.

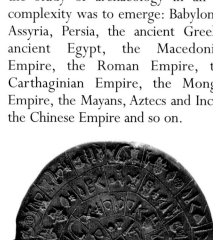

Above Early temples on Gozo, Malta, suggest the rise of a priestly elite.

Classical civilizations

Many archaeological chronologies now consist of a complex matrix of period, tool type, region and other cultural characteristics – codes that can seem complex to the non-specialist. Cutting across this complexity, however, are the monolithic terms that many of us are familiar with from the media – indeed, they are the classical civilizations and empires out of which the study of archaeology in all its complexity was to emerge: Babylonia, Assyria, Persia, the ancient Greeks, ancient Egypt, the Macedonian Empire, the Roman Empire, the Carthaginian Empire, the Mongol Empire, the Mayans, Aztecs and Incas, the Chinese Empire and so on.

Above Ancient Minoan records of grain, olive oil and dried fruit stores were inscribed on discs such as this one.

What distinguishes these cultures and empires is politics. Prehistorians tend to think about the societies they study as politically neutral – groups of roughly equal people co-existing and trading. However, complex stratified societies begin to emerge in the Neolithic era, in which some people are more equal than others – priests, potters and traders, for example. The Copper and Bronze Ages see the rise of hierarchical societies in which there is a growing difference between the homes of subsistence farmers living on what they can produce to feed and clothe themselves, and the palatial structures that mark out the elite – those who control mines, workshops or trade networks. Examples include some of the most famous of the world's archaeological sites, such as the palace of Knossos on Minoan Crete and the great cities of Ur, Uruk and Babylon.

The beginning of history

Associated with the rise of complex societies is the invention of writing and record keeping. Archaeologists make a distinction between proto-writing, which is the use of symbols (such as those found in ancient rock art, which convey information to those who have been initiated into their meaning) and writing systems consisting of signs that have a verbal or linguistic equivalent – each sign representing a vowel, consonant, syllable or word – and that follow the same grammatical rules as the spoken language.

Above The palace at Knossos was one of the largest Minoan palaces: in 1700BC, the whole complex contained some 14,000 rooms.

Right Was Stonehenge built by an egalitarian culture of co-operating families, or by a powerful leader using slaves or hired labour?

Above Tablets written in ancient Sumerian cuneiform script record the distribution of food.

The inventors of writing

To date, ancient Sumerians are acknowledged as the inventors of writing. This Bronze-Age culture of the late 4th millennium BC consisted of some 12 settlements in lower Mesopotamia (modern Iraq), each centred on a temple, and ruled by a king or priestly elite. Large numbers of records dating from 3500BC have been excavated from these temples. Written on clay tablets, in a script that later develops into cuneiform (meaning 'wedge-shaped', from the shape of the stylus used to form the letters), they relate to the storage and distribution of the city's food supplies.

Written records mark the essential boundary between what is considered archaeology and history. For many centuries, archaeology was thought to be an inferior tool for understanding the past – the blunt instrument that you used if no finer tool was available – and where archaeological evidence was used in the historical period, it was made to fit the written records. Only recently has archaeology begun to break away to the extent that archaeologists are now prepared to challenge what the history books say, and characterize much ancient history as fictional, poetic, dramatic, symbolic, rhetorical and biased – and not by any means a definitive and literal account of the past.

Today, the historian and the archaeologist bring different perspectives to this shared territory in which one studies written records and the other the material remains of the past to shed light on the complex cultures and civilizations of the past, their origins, rise, fall and demise, and the essential continuities that link them at the basic level of how ordinary people subsist and survive.

Ancient Civilizations

One way to try to come to terms with the sheer intricacy of complex stratified societies is to look at what was happening in different parts of the world at particular points in time to compare their technological development and social behaviour.

Around 3500BC, in the region known as Mesopotamia (Greek for 'between the rivers', referring to the fertile lands watered by the Rivers Tigris and Euphrates, now mainly in Iraq), city-states begin to develop, in which land and livestock were not owned by individuals, but were communally owned. They were managed by a governor or king, who also had a priestly function and lived in a complex that combined temple and palace.

Mesopotamian cities, such as Ur and Uruk, had populations of up to 65,000 people, and traded widely. The 'Royal Standard of Ur', found by British archaeologist Sir Leonard Woolley in the 1920s and dating from about 2600BC (now in London's British Museum), is a wooden box inlaid with scenes of war and peace made from shell and lapis lazuli from as far away as Afghanistan.

It is likely that Ur got its precious materials through trade with the walled towns of the valley of the Indus,

the longest and most important river in modern Pakistan, where the Harappan civilization (named after Harappa, one of the first Indus Valley settlements to be excavated) flourished from 3300 to 1900BC. Planned towns developed about 2600BC, with populations in the thousands and segregated residential and industrial areas, piped water, drains and sewers and houses built of standard-sized bricks, suggesting mass production and centralized control.

Other early developments

At about the same time, the potter's wheel was first invented in eastern China by the people of the Longshan culture, who are also noted for astonishingly delicate black vessels known as egg-shell pottery. In 2650BC in Egypt, the first pyramid was built (the Great Pyramid of Khufu), and in 2440BC in Europe the massive sarsen stone circle of upright stones capped by a lintel that we associate with today's

Above Some archaeologists argue that Olmec art suggests a strong link with African culture.

Stonehenge were erected – possibly using technology based on wheels or rollers. From pottery figurines found in graves in Mespotamia and the Indus Valley, we know that wheeled sledges and bullock carts were in use in Asia and India at this date.

In North America, the slow transition from a hunting and gathering society to farming is under way, but on the west coast of South America, the people of the Valdivia culture (modern Ecuador) are already farming maize, kidney beans, squash, cassava and peppers for food, and cotton plants for clothing and living in circular dwellings around a central plaza. They produced

Above Modern Iraq occupies the same lands as ancient Mesopotamia, known as the 'Cradle of civilization', from whose palace at Ur this statue was found.

Left The familiar profile of the Sphinx with the first pyramid of Khufu in the background.

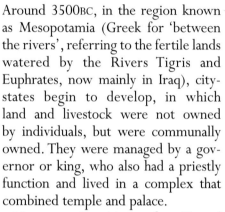

the earliest sculptures of the human figure yet found in the Americas and appear, from similarities in pottery styles, to be in contact with the ancient Jÿmon culture of Kyüshü, Japan – suggesting trans-Pacific trade.

From 2500 to 1250BC

The trends set in motion 1,000 years earlier – cities, long distance trade, writing and wheeled transport – are now part of world culture, in a swathe from the Pacific to the Atlantic, and Egyptian art, religion, prosperity and influence reach their height under the pharaohs. Minoan palace culture is established on the island of Crete with the building of the fresco-decorated palace at Knossos from 2000BC. Meanwhile, Chinese civilization as we know it today has its roots in the establishment of the Shang dynasty, with its hereditary rulers, fully developed writing systems, divination, astronomy, musical instruments and astonishing skill in casting ceremonial bronze vessels.

At 1500BC, boat-borne migrants known as the Lapita people begin to spread out from south-east Asia, travelling eastward to colonize the islands of the Pacific. In the Americas, there is evidence of similar long-distance sea and coastal journeys in the trade links between the people of the Great Lakes region in North America and those in Central America.

From 1250 to 500BC

The Olmec civilization of Mexico, believed to have been the progenitor of later Mesoamerican civilizations, such as the Maya, can be traced to cities and ceremonial centres established around 1200BC along the coast of Mexico, prospering on the trade in rare minerals used for toolmaking, including obsidian, basalt and jade. Metallurgy is the basis for wealth creation that accounts for the rise of the ancient Etruscans in Italy, the Phoenicians in north Africa and the people of mainland and island Greece. Long-distance trade is built on mastery of the sea, and the ancient Greeks

Right The ruins of Troy, whose story is told in Homer's *Iliad*, probably composed in the 8th century BC and one of earliest complete works of ancient literature to have survived.

develop mass-production techniques for building fast and manoeuvrable galleys, which proved an effective war machine in the constant battles that are depicted on their painted pottery. This decoration evolved from simple geometrical designs in the tenth millennium BC to depictions of Homeric epics 200 years later. Those epics, perhaps recorded from older oral poetry in the 8th century BC, tell of a historical conflict that dates from

City founders

A key debate in archaeology is the question of whether cities result from the decree of a single powerful leader or political entity ordering their construction, around a central palace or temple, or whether they arise from the organic growth of smaller groups or individuals who elect to live together. The theory of a singular leader as the catalyst for urbanization is reinforced by the Gilgamesh epic, the story of a powerful leader who built the city of Uruk, in what is today southern Iraq, the world's oldest named city.

Recent research carried out at Tell Brak, located in northern Mesopotamia (today's northern Iraq and north-eastern Syria) suggests that cities have more complex origins. The pattern of surface finds suggests that the city consisted of a central mound surrounded by settlement clusters. These clusters were separated from one another, indicating social distance among the groups. The patterns of settlement and distance from the central mound also signified autonomy from the political centre of the city.

between 1194BC and 1184BC, the dates of the major burning layers at the city of Troy (period VIIa). Warrior training and prowess are also the basis for the Olympic games, which were established in 776BC at the sanctuary of Zeus, in the ancient city of Olympia.

The books of the Old Testament date from this period, having been written down during the 11th to 2nd centuries BC, although describing events, such as the Exodus of the Jewish people from Egypt to the Promised Land, that probably took place between 1444 and 1290BC. However, the Jewish religion itself probably dates back further still – Abraham, the father of the Jewish people, is thought to have lived around 2000BC.

Measurement

Many cultures have contributed to the mathematical systems used as the basis for calendars, weights and measures. Evidence that humans first used fingers for counting comes from the fact that many numerical systems are based on patterns of tens. However, the ancient Sumerians used 60 as their base, which accounts for the 30 days of the month and the division of time into 60 seconds and minutes – these systems were adopted in ancient Egypt and passed to much of the Old World. Arabic numerals and the concept of zero were introduced to the West via trade between Europe and north Africa, but ultimately they derive from far older counting systems developed in India.

Ancient to Recent Past

From 500BC, the world as we know it today began to take shape. This is the era of emperors and heroes, but just as important is the role of religion in creating new forms of society, art and architecture, and of globalization — the merging of cultures that began with a voyage to the New World.

The Classical Age refers to the ancient Greek and Roman civilizations. Greece reached its peak in the 5th century BC, and in 336BC Alexander the Great of Macedon embarked on his conquest of the Persian Empire that led to the spread of Hellenic ideas from Greece to the borders of Tibet and India. The conquering Romans saw themselves as the heirs of Greek civilization, and adopted their deities, art and buildings styles. Virgil's national foundation myth – the *Aeneid* – mimics the ancient Greek poet Homer in its epic form and claims that Rome was founded by refugees from the burning city of Troy. At the peak of its power, the Roman Empire spread further still than Alexander's, its conquests stretching from Ireland in the west to the port towns of western India.

Just as importantly, these empires opened up trade routes along which ideas flowed as well as commodities,

and mystic eastern religions, including Mithraism and Christianity, challenged the cult of the emperor worship during the 1st and 2nd centuries AD. This led to the Edict of Milan (AD313), the decree of the Roman emperor Constantine the Great (c. 280–337) that established religious tolerance within the empire and ended the state persecution of Christians.

The Middle Ages

Constantine's reign marks the beginning of the Middle Ages in Europe – the intermediate period between the Classical Age and the Modern Era. It is a period in which religion has as big an impact on the archaeological record as the emperors and warriors of the

Above The Dharmarajika, Pakistan, one of the oldest stupas (dome-shaped Buddhist monuments or relic houses) in the world.

classical world, not only in Europe but all over the world, leading to new building types – the temples, mosques, monasteries and cathedrals that represent some of the oldest surviving monuments still in active use.

Although Hinduism (whose origins can be traced to the 3rd millennium BC), Zoroastrianism (16th century BC), Buddhism and Janeism (both 6th century BC) and Shinto (300BC) are all older than Christianity, it is not until the 1st century AD that these world religions begin to expand geographically and to make a significant mark

Above The Villa Adriana, Italy, the country palace of the Roman Emperor Hadrian.

Above Chichén Itzá, Yucatan, Mexico, seat of Mayan culture from 600–1000AD.

Left This medieval sculpture from Gandhara, Pakistan, shows knowledge of Roman classical art and suggests trade with the West.

Left This tobacco pipe symbolizes the post-Columban era when gold, potatoes and tobacco became the first New World exports.

in the archaeological record. Their expansion and influence are intimately connected to state sponsorship. It is with the adoption of these religions by leaders and elites that they spread and flower as major influences not just on the culture but also on the politics of the era. The so-called 'Donation of Constantine', the document in which the Roman emperor bequeathed his powers and territories to the Catholic Church and nominates the Pope as his heir, is now known to be a medieval forgery, but it typifies the connection between religion and politics that characterizes the Middle Ages in Europe. When Islam is founded by the followers of the holy prophet Muhammad (c. 570–632), it too makes no distinction between the religious and the political realms.

Similarly, the great cities of the Maya in Central America result from the fusion of religion and politics, constructed around pyramidal structures that serve both as religious centres and as the palaces of the Mayan rulers, including the renowned complex at Chichen Itza, which has its Asian counterpart in the stupendous Hindu (and later Buddhist) state temple and Khmer capital at Angkor Wat.

The Modern Era

Different cultures and people have different dates for when the Modern Era begins, but many scholars and university departments have adopted the date of 1500 as a convenient

Left This tobacco pipe symbolizes the post-Columban era when gold, potatoes and tobacco became the first New World exports.

starting point for what is variously called post-medieval or historical archaeology. The Modern Era has its roots in the Florentine Renaissance of the previous century, when scholars sponsored by the Medici family of bankers began to rediscover the works of ancient Greek and Roman authors by scouring the monasteries and libraries of Christian Europe as well as Islamic north Africa for forgotten manuscripts. The first crude excavations of Hadrian's villa and sites in Rome produced astonishing sculptures that had a profound effect on the art of the day, and on contemporary thinking, as Christian theologians began to absorb pagan classical ideals.

It was through this contact with the Islamic world, which until 1492 included the Emirate of Granada in southern Spain, that Europe learnt the mathematical and navigational ideas that underpinned their voyages of discovery and that led to that key watershed date of 1492, when Columbus and his crew undertook their five-week voyage across the Atlantic Ocean from the Canary Islands to the Bahamas.

Globalization

That one small voyage began the process of European expansion that characterizes the Modern Era. It is a process that has left a number of signatures in the archaeological record: including the large numbers of people who died from measles and smallpox imported from Europe to which they lacked immunity, the ubiquity of the clay pipes and the mass-produced ceramics that are found on sites from Australia to the Americas, and in the archaeology of the Transatlantic slave trade, where archaeologists in Africa, Europe and the Americas have sought to recover the evidence of a shameful period in our history.

Globalization has also had an important impact on archaeology. The roots of the discipline can be traced to the activities of 17th- and 18th-century antiquaries curious about the objects dug up from burial mounds or the ruins of ancient Greece and Rome, but the modern subject owes a great deal to the study of the many different people and cultures of the world. In fact, in some American universities, archaeology is not a separate subject, but one of four identified sub-disciplines of anthropology, the study of humanity.

Above The tomb of Columbus, Granada, Spain, honours the father of globalization.

Above Buddha statues recovered from the jungle which overran Angkor Wat, Cambodia.

Continental Africa

Nowhere else in the world can match Africa for the sheer longevity and diversity of its archaeology, nor for its range of contemporary cultures that have much to teach ethno-archaeologists about the diversity of people's art, beliefs and lifestyles.

Africa and archaeology are intertwined in many ways, and the discipline can trace many of its roots to the activities of Egyptologists who were sent out from European capitals to explore the ancient Nile. They often came back laden with the treasures that now fill many national museums – and not just mummies and temple facades. Some of the most fascinating finds from ancient Egypt are the everyday items that have survived remarkably unblemished, such as clothing, basketry and wooden furniture made during a period that saw the rise of Egypt as an international power, from 1550 to 1070BC.

Everyday life in Egypt

Thanks to its arid conditions, which help to preserve organic materials, ancient Egypt is still capable of surprising archaeologists, such as the discovery in 2006 of the timbers and rigging of the world's oldest sea-going vessels, dating from the middle of the second millennium BC, in caves at the Red Sea port of Marsa Gawasis. Stone anchors, limestone blocks, cedar and acacia wood beams, oar blades and over 80 perfectly preserved coils of different-sized ropes were discovered in the 4 caves. The extensive damage to the timbers by marine worms provided

Above Built in the 11th century, Great Zimbabwe has some of the oldest stone structures in Southern Africa.

clear evidence of their use as sea-going vessels, which disproved the long-held belief that the ancient Egyptians did not travel long distances by sea because of poor naval technology.

The sheer quantity and scale of Egyptian archaeological remains – such as the astonishing Great Pyramid of Giza, which was finished around 2560BC and is the only one of the Seven Wonders of the Ancient World – have so dominated our view of ancient Africa, that they led to the mistaken notion that the rest of the continent's past was backward and primitive.

However, even as Howard Carter was busy excavating the best-preserved pharaonic tomb ever found in the Valley of the Kings – that of Tutankhamun – over the winter of 1922 and 1923, German and British archaeologists were beginning to explore the fossil rich Olduvai Gorge in eastern Africa's Great Rift Valley, and their discoveries would soon open archaeologists' eyes to the African origins of the human race.

Bantu expansion

Accounting for the vast periods of time since the birth of toolmaking and hunter-gatherer society in Africa has proven to be a challenging task for archaeologists. However, underlying the complexity of the several hundred

Left Giza's Great Pyramid fascinated antiquaries and gave birth to Egyptian studies.

different peoples found in modern sub-Saharan Africa, they have detected a common language and culture, which is known as Bantu (a word that simply means 'the people' in many Bantu-derived languages).

As with the spread of agriculture in Europe and Asia, archaeologists argue over whether the physical migration of people led to the spread of the Bantu language and with it the adoption of farming from 7000BC and of copper-, bronze- and iron-working between 4000 and 500BC, or whether this knowledge was spread organically through contact with new ideas. Equally, there is much debate about the origins of Bantu culture, and whether it comes from south-eastern Nigeria, or further west, in Zambia and the Congo.

Aksum and Ethiopia

What is not in doubt is that the widespread adoption of farming, the use of iron for making tools and weapons, and of trade with Europe and Asia, led to the creation of some rich and powerful empires, such as the Aksumite Empire of northern Ethiopia and Eritrea.

It flourished from the 4th century BC and thrived on trade with Arabia, India and ancient Rome, exporting ivory, tortoiseshell, gold and emeralds, and trading in silk and spices. As well as its characteristic giant obelisks, used to mark the graves of its elite, the Aksumite civilization is best known for the frescoed rock-cut churches of such Ethiopian towns as Axum, Lalibela and Gondar, which resulted from the kingdom's adoption of Christianity around AD325.

Present-day Zimbabwe was the centre of another great empire from the 10th to 15th centuries AD. The ruins of the capital, Great Zimbabwe, once home to 18,000 people, are some of the oldest structures to survive in southern Africa; characteristic of the culture are dry-stone walled conical towers. The city controlled the main trading routes from South Africa to the Zambezi, where Arabic traders would come to buy locally mined gold, copper and precious stones, as well as animal hides, ivory and metal goods.

The slave trade and museum collections

Europe's determination to break the Asian monopoly on the trade in such luxury goods as gold, silver, silk, ivory, pepper and spices led to the first voyages of discovery in the 15th century and the beginnings of direct contact between sub-Saharan Africa and Europe. One tragic consequence was the expansion of the slave trade,

leading to what some archaeologists call the third 'out of Africa' diaspora, because slaves were shipped as a captive labour force first to the newly colonized islands of the Canaries and Madeira, then to the Caribbean and the Americas, and then to the European mainland. Slavery has itself now become a big subject of archaeological research, and because so few historical records survive, the excavation of sugar plantations is one way of recovering the facts about this shameful trade.

Treasures that have been acquired from Africa have helped to foster an appreciation of the often overlooked artistry and skill of Africans. However, they also present museums with an ethical dilemma, as the modern nations of the world ask for the return of cultural treasures that were taken from them in ways that are now considered unfair and unjust.

Above The rock-cut churches of Lalibela, Ethiopia, were inspired by Biblical accounts of the New Jerusalem, home to God and the saints.

Above Bantu oath-taking figure: Bantu languages and culture underlie the diversity of modern Africa.

Benin Bronzes

Colonial expansion by European powers into Africa led to one of history's great ironies: by conquest and looting, Europeans came to appreciate the African culture. The Benin Bronzes are an example. These detailed sculptures cast in the kingdom of Benin (today's central and northern Nigeria) from the 13th to the 16th centuries were taken by British forces in a 'Punitive Expedition' in 1897. They now occupy pride of place in many archaeological collections, such as that at the British Museum.

Left A ceremonial hip pendant worn by Benin chiefs.

Asia and Australasia

Asia is home to some of the oldest continuous civilizations, with cultures as varied as that of the Tamils of southern India, or of the Han people of China and as old as the ancient Greeks or Romans — yet their civilizations continue to thrive, where other dynasties and empires have passed into dust.

In the past, the focus of much archaeological research in Asia has been limited to the western regions (the ancient Near East), in modern Iran, Iraq, Turkey, Syria and in the Indus Valley region of what is now Afghanistan, Turkmenistan, Pakistan and western India. It is in these regions that agriculture, metallurgy, cities and settled state societies originated, along with the languages and writing and counting systems that are used by 62 per cent of today's world populations. Here, American and European archaeologists compete to claim older and still older evidence of the defining traits of civilization, but this pattern of research is slowly changing with the development of indigenous archaeological

Below The widely-studied archaeology of the Indus Valley includes some of the oldest and largest towns of the ancient world.

research programmes, which are showing what a melting pot of kingdoms, dynasties and religions this was.

Empires and religion

In India, it has been suggested that there is a continuity between the Indus Valley civilization of 3300BC and the Vedic period of the 2nd and 1st millennia BC. This is when the sacred Sanskrit texts known as the Vedas were composed, laying the foundation of Hinduism and the many independent kingdoms and republics that flourished from about 550BC, contemporary with Cyrus the Great (590–530BC), whose vast Persian Empire spread right to the Indus River.

Other great conquerors, such as Alexander the Great (356–323BC), the ancient Greek king of Macedon, also built extensive empires that reached to the borders of India. However, within

Above Terracotta warriors from the tomb of China's founder, Qin Shi Huang (died 210BC).

India itself, it was Ashoka (304–232BC) who united much of the subcontinent under one ruler and who embraced Buddhism, establishing schools and monasteries; he also placed moral ideals at the core of government. His model of kingship influenced the dynasties of southern India and many South-east Asian countries, including Cambodia, Laos, Myanmar (Burma), Thailand, and Vietnam, as did the twin influences of Hinduism and Buddhism.

The rich archaeological legacy of Angkor Wat, in Cambodia, results from this religious fusion, built in the 12th century AD as a temple to the Hindu deity Vishnu, and beautifully carved with scenes from the Hindu creation myth, then converted to Buddhist use in the 14th century.

The Chinese state

To the north, contemporary with Ashoka, Qin Shihuan (259–210BC) took an entirely different path to the unification of the vast Chinese Empire. Rather than encouraging diversity and tolerance in scholarship and religion, China's first emperor introduced the strong central control that continues to characterize China today — outlawing the ancient Chinese ethical and philosophical systems developed from the teachings of Confucius, with its humanistic emphasis on the civilized individual, and putting in its place the idea of the state as arbiter and the emperor as god. He was known to history as the initiator of such massive

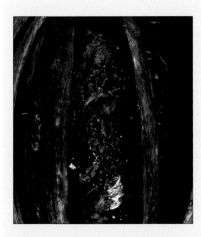

Frozen tombs of Siberia

The nomadic Pazyryk people of Siberia were merchants whose constant journeying on horseback along the trade routes connecting China to Europe from the 5th century BC is reflected in their art. Preserved by the permafrost of Siberia, their frozen tombs have yielded tattooed bodies, saddles, saddle bags, clothing, children's toys of felt, carpets and gilded wooden figurines, all of which demonstrate the assimilation of artistic ideas from the different people with whom they came into contact, from the Vikings of Scandinavia to the Buddhists and Hindus of Asia.

Above This distinctive Lapita pottery marks the cemeteries of the people who set out (perhaps from Vietnam, Taiwan or the Philippines) to colonize the Pacific islands from 1350BC.

infrastructural projects as the Great Wall of China and the national road system. It was not until 1974 that his greatest legacy, the terracotta army, was discovered, buried in a massive mausoleum in China's ancient capital, Xi'an. That underground army, found by farmers digging a well, is estimated

Above The triple lion monument of Ashoka the Great, adopted as India's national monument.

to be 8,000 strong, and is now the instantly recognizable international icon for China's past.

Nomads by sea and by land

These huge civilizations, builders of monuments that have become the basis of heritage-based tourism worldwide, can sometimes blind archeologists to the achievements of ordinary people, whose traces were barely visible in the archaeological record until the recent advent of DNA. This revealed the astonishing journeys that were made in the past, dispelling the belief that people were relatively immobile until the age of cars and aircraft.

For example, the Lapita people (named after the location of archaeological site on the Pacific island of New Caledonia, where their pottery was first recognized) travelled astonishing distances from about 1500BC to colonize the many tiny and remote islands of Oceania. Distinctive Lapita pottery is found in cemeteries on numerous South Pacific islands, buried with or underneath human remains. A distinctive feature of Lapita cemeteries is that the skulls of the deceased are often removed to a ceremonial house, and a shell is placed in the grave where the skull should be. Some of the graves also contain material that has been carried vast distances. A piece of the volcanic, glass-like stone called obsidian, used for toolmaking, was

found in a Fijian Lapita grave that had come from a mine on the island of New Britain in Papua New Guinea, some 4,500km (2,800 miles) to the west.

Modern Fijians have a myth that the descendants 'came from Africa', but the study of pig DNA tells a different story. The Neolithic colonizers of the Pacific carried pigs with them, and by comparing the genes of pigs from around the Asia-Pacific region, archaeologists have demonstrated that most of the region's pigs share a common ancestry, which can be traced to Vietnam. Other sources of evidence, including human genetic and linguistic data, support the idea that Pacific colonists first began their journey in Taiwan or the Philippines. This points to a steady migration eastward, with people moving from Vietnam along different routes through islands of South-east Asia, before fanning out on long oceanic journeys into the Pacific.

Long journeys by land and sea are by no means limited to the Lapita people. The Romani people were referred to as Gypsies based on the mistaken belief that they came from Egypt, but DNA studies have now established that they originated in the Punjab and Rajasthan regions of the Indian subcontinent, and that today's Romani, found all over Europe and North Africa, are the descendants of traders who have been journeying between Asia and Europe for more than 1,000 years.

The Americas

Daring seafaring journeys similar to those made by the Lapita people have brought people into the Americas. Others travelled long distances over a land bridge. However, exactly how and when these anonymous Asian people arrived remains the subject of research and considerable debate.

Most likely, many journeys were made rather than one. Some people travelled from Siberia, as big-game hunters tracked their quarry across the dried up Bering Strait and down the ice-free corridor east of the Rockies as the last glaciers began retreating about 13,000 years ago. Others came as seafarers out of the islands of Japan or the Pacific coasts of present-day Russia, hugging the coasts of Alaska and British Columbia as they hunted seals or harvested fish and seafood.

Some archaeologists believe there were even earlier journeys. A British-led team has found what it believes to be 40,000-year-old human footprints in New Mexico. Altogether 160 human footprints were found. Such an early date, derived from tests on the fossilized volcanic ash in which the footprints were found, has added to the tantalizing evidence from gene studies that links some of the people of southern America to indigenous Australians, suggesting that the first migrants to the Americas might have been seafarers from Australia.

The populous and sophisticated societies of pre-Columbian America were probably derived from fewer than 80 individuals, according to gene studies. Although that figure might seem small, bear in mind it probably represented just less than 1 per cent of the number of reproducing adults – about 9,000 – in northern Asia at the end of the ice age.

The rise of complex societies

Like their counterparts in Africa, Asia and Europe, these hunter-gatherer migrants developed agricultural systems. Squash and chilli were domesticated as early as 6000BC. Maize, beans and tomatoes soon followed, as did cotton, yucca and agave, all grown for textile fibres, and tree-borne fruits, including avocado, papaya and guava. Animal bones from food pits show that duck, deer and turkey were raised for meat, as were dogs, whose butchered bones are commonly found in middens dating from 3500BC onward.

Above Detail from the sinister 'games field' of Chichén Itzá, Mexico.

The availability of greater food resources through farming led to the rise of a sequence of complex and impressive cultures, especially in that area of Central America that stretches from Mexico to Costa Rica. This region saw the rise of some of the most advanced cultures of the Americas. They are grouped together as Meso-american cultures not just because they were geographical neighbours, but because they evidently shared ideas and innovations, including writing based on hieroglyphs, counting systems and formalized agricultural systems based on the movements of the sun, moon, planets and stellar constellations. They included the Olmec (1200BC to about 400BC) – which is sometimes described as the 'mother' culture for the later variants: the Teotihuacán (first millennium AD), the Maya (AD150–900), and the Aztec, Miztec and Zapotec (AD600 to the Spanish conquest of 1519).

Above Teotihuacán, the Aztec city in modern Mexico, was the biggest city in the Americas prior to European colonization.

Above The remnants in New Mexico of a settlement built by the Anasazi people (AD700–1130).

Above Excavating an American Indian site in Illinois, searching for evidence of trade, tools, weapons, religion, food and culture.

Above Machu Picchu was built in 1450, and its existence was only revealed to the wider world as recently as 1911.

The Lost City of the Incas

The story of Juanita, also known as the 'Ice Maiden', is that of a 14-year-old girl whose frozen remains were discovered on top of Mount Ampato near Arequipa, Peru, in 1995. Sacrificed around 1445, she is the best preserved of many young children offered to the gods, perhaps because of their purity, by the Inca people. Their empire arose from the highlands of Peru in the early 13th century and, through conquest and assimilation, grew to incorporate a large portion of western South America. Within a few years of the arrival of the Spanish conquistadors in 1532, Inca culture was dead, ravaged by war with the Spanish, and then by smallpox, typhus, flu, diphtheria and measles.

Those few who survived continued to farm the slopes of Machu Picchu meaning 'the Old Peak', and often referred to as 'the Lost City of the Incas'. Lost only to the outside world, it was 'rediscovered' in 1911 by Hiram Bingham, who was shown the secret route to the site by local people, paving the way for this icon of Inca civilization to be designated as a World Heritage Site in 1983 and become the most visited tourist attraction in Peru. Today, Macchu Picchu illustrates many of the dilemmas that face archaeologists when a site becomes too popular. Visitors and film crews have caused damage to the site, and there is pressure from developers who want to construct a cable car to the ruins, to develop a luxury hotel, shop and restaurant complex and to build a helicopter landing pad. Despite this, the remoteness of Macchu Picchu in the slopes of the Andes, retains its power to evoke a sense both of human insignificance and of the astonishing lengths to which humans have gone to form and shape the world.

Mesoamerican life

Religion and symbolism permeated all aspects of Mesoamerican life, and archaeologists are still discovering the many ways in which buildings and landscape were shaped as a symbolic mirror of the real and mythical cosmos. For example, cities were aligned on the cardinal points of the compass and divided into a northern zone, which was the realm of the underworld where tombs are found, and a southern zone, with its markets and residential zones for the living. At the axis of the two zones, the monumental plaza, with its governmental buildings, defined the crossing point between the two worlds. Towering pyramids topped by temples reach to the heavens.

Long narrow L-shaped ball courts, with high side-walls, were the setting for some form of ritual game. The rules are unknown, but it is thought they might have involved human sacrifice — whether the winners, the losers or all of the participants lost their lives to the gods is far from clear. Plenty of finds demonstrate that human lives were sacrificed to the gods, and one of the great debates in Mesoamerican

archaeology is the degree to which warfare and violence were implicated in the rise and often sudden demise of empires and dynasties.

If violence was implicated in the collapse of the city of Teotihuacán around AD750 or of the decline of the Mayan civilization from between AD800 and 1000, was it internal conflict, political, social or religious upheaval or attack from an external enemy? What is clear of course is that

Above The jungle still hides many Mayan sites, like the remains of this house in Aguateca, Guatemala, founded around AD100.

in every case it was the political and religious structures that collapsed. Ordinary people went on surviving, adapting and living in the world that might even have been regarded as a better place without priests and rulers calling for blood letting and sacrifice from time to time.

Case study: Çatalhöyük

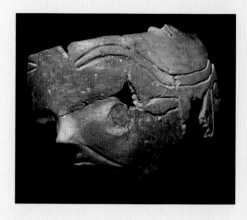

Archaeologists in the 19th century presented our prehistoric ancestors as crude, brutish and inarticulate. The excavation of the Neolithic settlement of Çatalhöyük in modern Turkey, reveals just how far from the truth this equation is between prehistoric and primitive.

Archaeologists derive much of their information about the origins of agriculture, houses, cities and societies from the excavation of hillocks or mounds called 'tells', that might look natural at first but that are really the result of the accumulation of debris from thousands of years of human occupation on the site. Tells, when excavated, consist largely of the remains of the collapsed mud-brick walls of houses, temples and public buildings, but also of hearths, debris and industrial areas, which archaeologists have systematically excavated, looking for, and finding, the origins of early agricultural communities.

There are some 50,000 visible tells in Asia alone, testifying to the long settlement of the area. Tells are found as far east as the Indus Valley and as far west as Turkey, where the name for such a mound is höyük, as in Çatalhöyük, which means 'Fork Mound', the renowned Neolithic site in central Turkey, south-east of the present-day city of Konya.

Rooftop access

Occupied between 7400 and 6000BC, Çatalhöyük's mud-brick houses are so tightly packed that there are no streets. Rooftops served as a public plaza and people gained access to their homes by climbing down ladders. Each home consisted of a main room for working, cooking, eating and sleeping, and side rooms for storage and food preparation, and each housed a family of five to ten people.

Above One of the Neolithic pots excavated at Çatalhöyük, displaying faces.

Houses were kept scrupulously clean, and the mud-brick walls were coated in white plaster. Refuse was deposited in pits outside the home, and excavating these reveals that wild food (fish, waterfowl and eggs and wild cattle) was a major source of meat for the community, in addition to domesticated sheep and cattle. Food remains from storage bins reveal that wheat, barley and peas were grown, and almonds, pistachios and fruit were harvested from orchards. Pottery and obsidian tools were manufactured, and traded for dates from the Levant, sea shells from the Mediterranean or Red Sea and flint from Syria.

Left Archaeologists restore the red paint daubed on a wall on 'Building 59'.

Above An elevated view of one of the buildings in the southern portion of the site.

Rich symbolism

However, what the excavation also reveals is the extent to which ritual and symbolism dominated people's lives. Instead of religion being concentrated in special buildings, every house seems to have doubled up as a shrine and cemetery. The walls were painted with hunting scenes and images of aurochs (wild cattle), leopards and vultures swooping down on headless figures. The heads of animals, including large horned bulls, were mounted on the walls, where they must have been a constant inconvenience, with their thrusting horns taking up limited interior space.

Stranger still, the people of Çatalhöyük lived with their deceased relatives all around them. The dead were buried in pits beneath hearths and under sleeping platforms, often placed in baskets or wrapped in reed mats. The skulls were occasionally dug up and given plaster faces, painted to recreate eyes and flesh and the appearance of living human flesh.

Every so often the houses themselves were ritually dismantled, leaving just the lower 90cm (3ft) or so of the original walls, which were then filled in with demolition rubble, sometimes taking great care to bury the domed clay oven and hearth in such a way as to protect it from damage. Objects such

Above The inhabitants buried at Çatalhöyük were often wrapped in woven artefacts, which helped archaeologists to date the remains.

as stone axes and bone tools were deliberately buried in the fill and in the walls of the new home, as were female figurines modelled in clay or carved from horn and various types of stone. Similar carvings were also placed in food and grain storage bins.

Experimental archaeology

The current excavations at Çatalhöyük, which began in 1993 under the leadership of Ian Hodder (then of the University of Cambridge, now of Stanford University), have been described as the most ambitious excavation projects currently in progress anywhere in the world, partly because the excavators are seeking to pioneer new approaches to excavation in which everyone taking part can contribute to decision-making and to the interpretation of the site. In this sense, the excavation mirrors the structure of the original Çatalhöyük community, which appears to have been democratic to the extent that there are no obvious buildings that can be identified as palaces or temples. The population of Çatalhöyük – up to 8,000 people at any one time – seem to have lived together as genuine equals.

Above A child's skeleton – dated to the later phase of the settlement's history – lies in one of the burial 'hearths'.

Ian Hodder says of the site: 'a child growing up in such a household would soon learn how the space was organized – where to bury the dead and where to make beads, where to find the obsidian cache and where to place offerings. Eventually, he or she would learn how to rebuild the house itself. Thus the rules of society were transferred not through some centralized control, but through the daily practices of the household.'

This is a site that challenges how archaeologists explain the mindset of Neolithic people, and some have said that it is not typical. Yet there are echoes all over the region of similar practices, especially in the female figurines and in the references to bulls (in Greek legend, the people of Europe are descended from Europa). The more sites archaeologists excavate from this period and in this region, the more evidence is discovered for a cult of skulls and for rituals involving dangerous animals, such as wild cattle, wild boar, leopards, snakes and scorpions. It is a curious paradox that such threatening creatures should be associated with the beginnings of domestication and the taming of nature.

SPECIALISMS

Given that archaeology is the study of the material remains of the human past, it follows that all artefacts – physical objects made by human hands – have an archaeology. Archaeologists can identify the earliest known book (as distinct from scrolls or writing tablets), for example, to 3rd-century Egypt (the so-called Gnostic manuscripts, found in 1945 buried in a jar near the Nile). They can use archaeological techniques to date the wooden boards, leather, textiles and paper from which books are made, they can study the techniques employed in their construction and they can excavate workshops or monastic scriptoria where they were made. Archaeology is, thus, a discipline with as many possible subjects as there are archaeologists willing to research them. There are major branches of the subject with a substantial body of literature; most of these specialisms have societies and journals dedicated to providing a forum for specialists to share their techniques and discoveries, and all of them can be studied at university.

Opposite Archaeologists specializing in Polynesian culture prepare to move the famous Easter Island monoliths.

Above Students of buildings' archaeology use a planning frame to record the outer stone structure of a medieval mill.

Above Specialists examine fragments of papyrus – an ancient writing material made from the pith of plants.

Above Archaeologists in Hanoi, Vietnam, restore the excavated ruins of an ancient citadel dating from the 7th century AD.

Industrial Archaeology

The term 'industrial archaeology' is used to mean the study of mining, manufacturing, transport and the other large-scale processes that are associated with the Industrial Revolution. Its origins can be traced to the 16th century, but industrial processes flourished from the late 18th century.

Instead of studying romantic ruins set in beautiful landscapes and excavating small-scale sites to find delicate traces of people living in the natural environment, industrial archaeologists study the remains of processes that left ugly scars across the landscape, reduced human beings to slavery as adjuncts of machines, caused disease, injury and death and have left a legacy of pollution and climate change across the planet. Unsurprisingly, industrial archaeologists have struggled for recognition – it is more challenging to persuade people that a redundant steel works or coal mine represents an important part of our heritage than a medieval abbey.

Industrial accomplishments

Since the 1950s, archaeologists have had an impact by standing up for the preservation and restoration of railways and canals and for the reuse of industrial buildings as loft-style apartments. They have persuaded UNESCO to recognize as World Heritage Sites some of the places that mark milestones in industrial history: in Great Britain these include the Blaenavon Industrial Landscape in south Wales, where steel making was invented; the Cornwall and West Devon Mining Landscapes, where deep-mining techniques were developed that are now practised all over the world; and New Lanark, in Scotland and Saltaire, in Yorkshire, as examples of model industrial towns where mill workers were given decent houses, clean water and education, in contrast to the exploitation they commonly experienced elsewhere. They have also encouraged the study of large landscapes and the connections between the different processes.

Above Excavating large industrial sites usually requires a tentative partnership between manpower and machinery.

Pioneers at Ironbridge

The Ironbridge Gorge landscape, in Shropshire, England, also a World Heritage Site, is an exemplar. It has been dubbed the birthplace of the Industrial Revolution because it was here that Abraham Darby I (1678–1717) perfected the smelting process that opened up an era of cheap iron (later used so effectively by his grandson, Abraham Darby III, who built the famous iron bridge after which the gorge is named in 1779).

When archaeologists studied the area in the 1970s, they pioneered techniques for documenting and preserving the entire community, with all its inter-related activities. They also created a

Above Ironbridge Gorge, birthplace of the Industrial Revolution, survives as an outdoor museum.

Above The Industrial Revolution was built on coal and iron from deep mines, brought to surface by pit head winding gear.

Above Parts of an industrial press for bending and shaping metal from a Russian steelworks.

Finding out more
There are national and regional organizations for people who share an interest in their industrial past. All three organizations listed below offer annual conferences, journals and publications, as well as study tours and links with local and regional groups undertaking practical work in the field.
• Great Britain, the Association for Industrial Archaeology: www.industrial-archaeology.org.uk
• United States, the Society for Industrial Archaeology: www.sia-web.org
• Australia, New Zealand and the Asia-Pacific region, Australasian Society for Historical Archaeology: www.asha.org.au

new form of open-air museum, with multiple sites, as evidence of the messiness and complexity of the region's quarrying, iron-making and ceramic manufacturing industries, but also of the social consequences, preserving examples of workers' housing, shops, chapels and educational institutes. Ironbridge set an example that was rapidly taken up all over the world, and industrial archaeology is now a global activity.

In general, industrial archaeology involves recording landscapes, buildings, machinery and processes, by means of still photography and video film, measured drawings and written descriptions. Industrial archaeologists might record a specific industrial

Below This horse-drawn engine replicates ancient mining conditions in the Wieliczka Salt Mines in Poland.

complex, such as Isambard Kingdom Brunel's 1840s railway works at Swindon, in Wiltshire, the factory for the world's first commercial railway, the Great Western Railway, or they might be interested in a specific building type – for example, studies have recently been published on naval dockyards, gunpowder factories, breweries, cotton mills and glassworks, seeking to write the history of an industry through its surviving physical remains.

Human knowledge

A future challenge for the discipline is not just to record redundant buildings and machinery, but also to capture the skills of people who still have the knowledge to keep the machines running and explain how they work. Much effort in industrial archaeology today is spent in gathering data in the form of interviews and video recordings of people working in those countries where historic industrial processes can still be found: Bessemer

(a process named after the English inventor Henry Bessemer) and open-hearth steel-making, long extinct in Sheffield, where the processes were developed, but still practised in the Urals, for example, or textile manufacture in and around Mumbai, using processes that Mahatma Ghandi saw in England in the 1890s but that have long ago disappeared from there.

Industrial archaeology commands political attention because it represents the heritage of many people alive today: people who themselves worked in coal mines, factories or steelworks, or those whose parents and grandparents did. This adds resonance and meaning to industrial heritage, but enormous challenges are involved in preserving industrial heritage and presenting it in any meaningful way because of the scale of industrial monuments, and the costs involved.

In Europe, one solution is the creation of the European Route of Industrial Heritage (ERIH), a network of important industrial sites that have left their mark on European industrial history and that are thought important enough to warrant government funding. At a global level, the International Committee for the Conservation of the Industrial Heritage (TICCIH) has been formed to promote the study, protection, conservation and explanation of the remains of industrialization, and their aims are set out in the Nizhny Tagil Charter for Industrial Heritage of 2003. Its website – www.mnactec. com/TICCIH – is a good starting point for anyone interested in learning more about the subject.

Coastal and Marine Archaeology

Water, although a difficult medium to work in, can be an excellent medium for preserving archaeological remains, from wrecked ships to drowned villages. Finding, excavating and preserving such remains requires a repertoire of highly specialized skills.

Above Recovering the anchor from Henry VIII's sunken flagship the *Mary Rose*.

The discovery of prehistoric villages beneath the lakes of Switzerland and Italy and at Mere, near Glastonbury in Somerset, England, alerted archaeologists as far back as the late 19th century to the exceptional state of preservation that exists in waterlogged sites. The absence of free oxygen in such sites excludes those bacteria that cause organic materials to rot and fade from the archaeological record. These 'anaerobic' or 'anoxic' sites, as they are called, are rich in the objects that give us a much more complete picture of daily life in the past, including

Below Archaeologists at Baia Bay, Italy, recover a marble couch that was once part of the Emperor Claudius's summer home.

complete human bodies – the so-called 'bog people' found in peat deposits in northern Europe.

Special excavation methods

Finding, excavating and preserving such remains requires a repertoire of highly specialized skills. In some cases, the site to be excavated can be drained of water by surrounding it with a coffer dam and pumping the water out. Such sites are often sprayed continually with water, or flooded again at the end of every day. Because stepping on the site will damage precious organic remains, as will the use of the digger's normal repertoire of metal barrow, pick, spade and trowel, the diggers are suspended above the remains on planks, lying

Above Divers survey a ship wrecked in 1025AD at Serçe Limani, Turkey, dubbed the 'Glass Ship', because of the large quantity of glass found in the vessel's cargo.

(uncomfortably) on their stomachs to excavate preserved timbers using plastic spatulas.

Organic finds begin to deteriorate as soon as they are exposed to air, so conservation is a high priority, with artefacts and ecofacts being placed in water tanks for immediate treatment, and eventually being preserved by careful drying and stabilization. In some cases, this involves the slow and expensive process of replacing the water content with wax. Such efforts are rewarded by the quality, nature and completeness of the finds assemblages from waterlogged sites, such as the 1,000 letters written on birch bark found at Novgorod in Russia that tell so much about daily in the city about AD1400, or the leather shoes from London that tell us about medieval fashions, or the beautiful silk cap imported from central Asia that was worn by a Viking settler in York, in the north of England, in the 10th century.

Working underwater

Compared with working on waterlogged sites, working on underwater sites is more challenging still. Even sites lying in only a few feet of water demand diving skills and expensive specialist equipment. Sites further from land need a boat or ship to provide a means of access and support for the activities being undertaken in the water, as well as facilities for conservation. Weather, tides, strong currents and limited visibility provide

Above Late medieval shoes recovered from a waterlogged site in excellent condition.

Above A diver surveying the remains of the *Mary Rose* underwater.

Mary Rose

Completed in 1511, the *Mary Rose* sank during an engagement with the French fleet in 1545. Her rediscovery and excavation from 1979 led to the pioneering of many techniques now commonly used on similar projects worldwide, as has her lifting from the sea bed on an iron frame on 11 October, 1982. This marked the beginning of a decades-long conservation project to preserve the remains of the hull and the many possessions of the crew that were found on board. These include musical instruments, games, quill pens and inkwells, leather-bound books, navigational and medical equipment, carpentry tools, guns, longbows, arrows, cooking and eating utensils and lanterns.

an ever-changing and often dangerous work environment, but maritime archaeologists are not easily deterred and have developed survey and recording techniques that enable them to overcome such hazards. Unlike commercial salvagers who look for a quick return for their efforts, underwater archaeologists record everything they find – just like a terrestrial archaeologist – even if the process takes far longer and is more costly, because it involves expensive electronic measuring tools.

The history of the ship

Underwater archaeology has long been associated with the finding of historic shipwrecks – from the *Titanic* to the *Mary Rose* – and many maritime archaeologists specialize in the study of vessel construction and use, based on the wrecks they can excavate and lift. Not all of them involve diving. The oldest boat yet found, a plank-built vessel used for river transport 4,000 years ago, was found protruding from the peat and clay banks of the River Humber, at North Ferriby in Yorkshire, northern England, while the world's oldest known seagoing vessel, a Bronze Age boat from 1000BC, came from a deep waterlogged hole in the middle of Dover, the coastal town in south-east England. In Pisa, Italy, 16 ancient ships, complete with cargo, ropes, fishing equipment and stone anchors, were found a few hundred metres from the Leaning Tower in the silted up channel of a former river bed.

By contrast, hundreds of Spanish, French, English and American ships lie in waters of varying depth around

Finding out more

The following societies and institutes provide training in maritime arachaeology, from one-day introduction courses to advanced diving and archaeology studies:
• Great Britain, the Nautical Archaeology Society brings together professional and amateur archaeologists: www.nasportsmouth.org.uk
• Great Britain, Bristol University: www.bris.ac.uk/archanth/postgrad/maritime.html
• United States, the Institute of Nautical Archaeology based at Texas A&M University: ina.tamu.edu
• United States, the Lighthouse Archaeological Maritime Program (LAMP) in Florida: www.staugustinelighthouse.com/lamp.php
• Australia, Flinders University: ehlt.flinders.edu.au/archaeology/specialisations/maritime

the coastline of both sides of the Atlantic, evidence of European global exploration, the formation of colonial empires, and the development of trans-Atlantic economy. The port of Cádiz in Spain, which played such a key role in the Spanish colonization of the South American continent, is estimated to be the grave for no less than 800 ships that went to the bottom of the sea during the 16th to 18th centuries. The Nautical Archaeology Society has records of an amazing 40,000 historic ship losses around Great Britain's coast, but estimates that there are at least 60,000 more.

Some wrecks are of value to archaeologists because of their cargoes, and some because of what they might

reveal about naval architecture and shipbuilding technology, while others have immense historical value. For example, the *Bonhomme Richard*, the 42-gun frigate commanded by John Paul Jones, America's naval hero, who daringly brought the battle right to the shores of his enemy during the war of the American Revolution, winning America's first ever naval victory against a nation that had previously commanded the seas. Scuttled after the battle, Jones's flagship, *Bonhomme Richard*, lies somewhere off the English coast at Flamborough Head, east Yorkshire, where the Naval Historical Center in Washington and the Ocean Technology Foundation are currently scanning the ocean floor to find it.

Churches

Any building that has been altered since its original construction has an archaeology, because its history can be divided into different phases of construction. In the case of churches, some of which are nearly 2,000 years old, that archaeology can be complex.

Churches are among the world's oldest standing buildings. The earliest churches in Europe stand on the sites of pagan temples, and incorporate Roman buildings into their crypts. By the Middle Ages, every parish community in Europe has a church, and most have survived to the present. Churches are not restricted to Europe. Some of the world's oldest churches survive in the Holy Land, in Egypt and Ethiopia, and in parts of Turkey, Syria, Lebanon, Jordan and Georgia – some of them converted to mosques, some surviving as remote rural churches or monasteries.

Over the centuries that have passed since these churches were constructed, they have been altered, remodelled and improved many times, in order to accommodate changing ceremonies and religious ideas, to cope with growing congregations, to keep up with the latest architectural fashion, or to incorporate the chapels and memorials of wealthy donors. Rarely is the church razed to the ground and rebuilt; more often the adaptation affects only part of the building, so that older parts survive, perhaps hidden under plaster or pierced by new windows, arches or doors.

Stratigraphy and style

Unravelling the precise sequence in which the church was built and altered is the challenge that faces church archaeologists, who use techniques like those of the terrestial archaeologist. A church (or any other multi-phase building for that matter) can be analysed by its stratigraphy, using logic to determine that one area of masonry must be older than another because of the way one area overlies the other or is bonded or abutted to it. Just as artefacts can be placed in chronological series, buildings can be phased on the basis of their stylistic details.

Most people are familiar with the names and rough dates of the broad categories of European architecture – classical, Romanesque, Gothic, Renaissance, Baroque, Neo-Gothic, Eclectic, Arts and Crafts and Modern –

but these are broad categories that architectural historians and building archaeologists have been studying and refining for some 300 years. The results of all that research are what enable an experienced church archaeologist to walk around a church, analysing the patterns and discontinuities in the exterior and interior walls and noting diagnostic architectural details, and make a good stab at giving the history of the building and the main phases of its construction and alteration.

New discoveries

Given that churches, from magnificent cathedrals and majestic monasteries to humble rural chapels, have been studied for so long, and given that nearly all of them now have written histories, one might ask whether there is anything left to learn. Most church archaeologists would say that the amount we do not know far exceeds the amount we do know, partly because many of the diagnostic details that enable church archaeology to be studied are hidden in places that are not normally accessible – high up in the soaring roof space or beneath the soil of the church floor – or are disguised by plasterwork or later masonry.

Church archaeology comes into its own once a church is subject to a major restoration programme that might include the introduction of scaffolding or the removal of floors or plasterwork – but the floors and plasterwork might

Above 12th-century San Joan de Casselles church, Andorra, served the spiritual needs of medieval pilgrims.

Above The medieval church at Berkeley Castle, Gloucestershire, UK, might have been built on top of a Saxon palace and nunnery.

themselves be of great archaeological interest and so should never be removed without prior study.

The Tomb of Christ

The importance of studying structures in situ is demonstrated in the restoration of the Rotunda of the Anastasis (the Resurrection), in the Church of the Holy Sepulchre in Jerusalem. It stands over a rock-cut tomb discovered by workers employed by the Roman emperor Constantine the Great in AD325, and has been revered since as the Tomb of Christ.

When the comparatively modern marble structure placed over the site of the Sepulchre was found to be bulging under the weight of its superstructure and in imminent danger of falling down, archaeologist Martin Biddle was allowed to study the structure in minute detail. He found numerous earlier structures, which he compared to an onion, one surviving inside the next. This enabled him to reconstruct the appearance of the tomb at various stages in history, including those periods when medieval pilgrims and Crusader Kings flocked to the Holy Land to visit the Sepulchre. Biddle also examined the remains of the original rock-cut tomb, which he identified as part of a 1st-century BC quarry, re-used as a Jewish cemetery in the 1st century AD. It was the site of a public building — a temple — built after Titus destroyed the city of Jerusalem after the Jewish Revolt of AD70.

This temple, perhaps dedicated to the Roman goddess Aphrodite, was

Below The first church built in the United States, at Jamestown, Virginia.

itself destroyed by Constantine's agents in AD325 as they searched for Calvary or Golgotha, the site of Christ's crucifixion, and the tomb identified as the place of his resurrection. To protect these holy places, Constantine then built the first in a series of magnificent Christian buildings, which have themselves been adapted, altered and repaired many times following their initial construction.

The lessons that emerge from many such exercises in unpeeling the onion of church history is that many such buildings are much older than they look, and that many have hidden

Above The masonry of walls and windows may offer clues as to construction dates.

Above A specialist inspects worn stone on Notre Dame Cathedral in Paris, as part of a ten-year restoration project.

Petrological analysis

Based on the assumption that builders use different materials each time they modify, adapt or extend a building, the history of a building can be revealed by petrological analysis. By examining the structure, it can show a change of stone size or type, or a change in construction technique, from large square-cut stones to small rectangular stones, or from stones laid in a regular pattern to those laid randomly. The methods of construction used for window or door openings can also be dated precisely: for example, the use of small flat stones and tiles set in a hemispherical arch, or the use of a single stone as a lintel. The history of a building can thus be analysed by recording the place, shape and position of the materials making up the fabric of the wall, and their geological type.

This technique, when used to study the eastern wall of the Saxon church at Deerhurst, in Gloucestershire, in the west of England, revealed a patchwork of 19 different types of stone, from the earliest Saxon masonry at the bottom of the wall, to the evidence of roof heightening and restoration work carried out in the 19th century. What interested archaeologists was the evidence of two triangular shapes high up on the wall, which led to the discovery of two panels on the interior with the faint signs of paintwork and of a figure scratched into the stone. Although only visible now under special lighting conditions, the lines were made by a 10th-century artist setting out the outlines before painting in the detail of what would have been vividly coloured saintly figures set in triangular niches.

histories that have yet to emerge. Sometimes, simply turning over a stone can reveal a new chapter to the building's history. This is exactly what happened when church archaeologist Warwick Rodwell was finishing a six-week excavation of the floor of Lichfield Cathedral, in the English Midlands, when a piece of masonry

was lifted to reveal, hidden on the underside, a beautifully carved angel, now known to be part of an 8th-century shrine to the cathedral's founder, St Chad, with much of its original painted decoration still intact. This find gives valuable insights into the possible appearance of the first Saxon church on the site.

Buildings

Some of the techniques used in church archaeology apply to any old or multi-period building, but archaeologists in this field use a huge range of other techniques, involving timber joints and tree-ring dating, door and window styles, brick sizes and bonding techniques and even paint analysis.

If you invite a house 'detective' into your home to analyse its structure, he or she will probably head straight to the attic, because this is where the tell-tale signs are often found that offer clues to the age of the house. Looking at the timbers that hold up the roof and keep the house dry, an archaeologist will gain some idea of the date from the wood itself – whether it is sawn or split, whether it is a relatively modern material, such as pine, or an older local wood, such as oak, chestnut or elm – from the type of truss (the structural framework of wood used to support the rafters and roofing material) and the joints used to join together the different timbers making up the truss.

Other clues include the thickness of the timbers – and whether they are from the branches of the tree or from the main trunk – whether there is any decorative work that might suggest the timbers were intended to be seen as the open roof of a hall, and whether there is any soot or smoke blackening – often the sign of an early house without a chimney. Of course, all of these features can be found, but will not necessarily date your house, because timber was a valuable resource that was often recycled. A buildings archaeologist will look for a range of clues and some degree of consistency – there is always the possibility that recycled timbers came from an earlier house on the same site.

Right When examining walls, archaeologists carefully look for clues that indicate where extensions have been added or alterations made at a later date to the original building.

Truss typology and dateable details

A buildings archaeologist can speak with confidence about dates based on analysing the roof trusses because many years of study by local architectural societies have established that roof trusses and jointing techniques have changed and evolved at regular intervals, depending on fashion, the availability of raw materials and the status of the house. Many of these changes are regional in character – such as the style of the carved ornamentation on door frames, for example, while some are national in character, such as the dimensions of standard house bricks at different periods in time, and the different patterns used for laying those bricks.

Once the dating of such features was broad and approximate, because it depended on being able to date the main construction phases of the building on the basis of written records – letters, diaries, leases, deeds and inventories. However, tree-ring dating (*see* Dendrochronology and Other Dating Methods) is now commonly employed to give much more precise dates to diagnostic features.

Above One of the main objectives of rescue projects is to make a record for posterity of buildings facing demolition.

Specialists within the field

There are some buildings archaeologists who specialize in the field known as vernacular architecture, which is the study of ordinary people's homes, how they developed and what those houses can tell us about living conditions in the past. Yet others specialize in studying the development of a particular building type – be it farmsteads, hospitals, prisons, silk mills, town halls, cinemas, theatres or railway stations. However, perhaps the biggest field of work for those who make a living from the study of buildings is in understanding and conserving what are termed 'polite' buildings, which often take the form of large public buildings, the grand houses of the aristocracy or historic monuments,

Below The depth of a roof beam can be a clue to its age: medieval beams were bigger because large trees were plentiful, but shipbuilding and warfare rapidly reduced the availability of mature timber.

Above 18th-century Kew Palace, London, was restored using clues from scraps of original paint and fabric surviving in attics and behind later panelling.

such as medieval castles. Many of these are owned by charitable bodies and are open to the public, and their care, conservation and presentation to the public depends on a detailed understanding of their archaeology.

From studying the structure of the building, it is possible to write a detailed history of which parts are the oldest, and what was added or changed over time. Tying those changes into written records then adds a human dimension. Arachaeologists might be able to say who built the library, as well as when. Buildings archaeology can be dry without a vivid sense of what that castle or stately home actually looked like at different stages in its history, and to understand this buildings archaeologists can literally 'excavate' the walls for tiny patches of surviving decorative surfaces by peeling away the different layers of paint, plaster or wallpaper to build up a dated sequence of decorative schemes.

Restoring Kew Palace

One recent example was the ten-year restoration of Kew Palace, in west London, which was completed in 2006. Although called a palace, this was a relatively small and intimate home

that served as a country retreat for the royal family in the late 18th century. It was built on the edge of a former royal park, which was developed into the Royal Botanic Gardens when the park was used for planting the many exotic plant specimens that British explorers sent back from their travels in Africa and Australasia.

Astonishingly, large parts of the palace remained untouched from since the time of King George III and Queen Charlotte (1800–1818), so it was possible to piece together the decorative scheme of 1804 by studying small flakes of paint and scraps of paper and fabric that had survived beneath later panelling. Where these had lost their original colour due to fading and ageing, a battery of scientific techniques, including chemical analysis and polarized light microscopy, were used to analyse the minerals and dyes employed in paints and furnishings.

The attics in particular yielded paint finds going back to the very first merchant's house of 1631 that was enlarged to create the palace. To show how the historically authentic decorative schemes were researched, one room has been left in its original state, unrestored, to enable visitors to see the evidence for themselves and compare the room as found with the vibrantly colourful bedrooms, library, boudoirs and reception rooms of the rest of the palace.

Above Vermont State House, United States, was painstakingly restored in the 1980s.

Vermont State House

Another classic example of archaeology coming to the aid of a building restoration programme can be seen in the richly arrayed interiors of the Vermont State House, home to the government of the American state of Vermont. This is a fine example of Greek Revival architecture that opened in 1859 and was carefully restored in the 1980s. One of the challenges in building restoration is to decide which of the many decorative schemes in the history of a building should be given priority. In this case, rather than return all the rooms back to one point in time, the archaeologists recovered evidence for over a century of changing fashions and tastes, from the original Neoclassical style, to American Empire, Renaissance Revival, Rococo Revival and Aesthetic Movement.

Finding out more
The following websites are useful for buildings archaeology:
- Great Britian, the Institute of Historic Buildings Conservation: www.ihbc.org.uk
- United States, the National Trust for Historic Preservation: www.nationaltrust.org

Forensic Archaeology

In this emerging science, forensic archaeologists collect evidence for recent criminal investigations – especially in cases involving murder, genocide and war crimes – and also to solve ancient puzzles, such as the identity of Jack the Ripper or the cause of Beethoven's death.

When human remains need to be excavated in ways that will enable the maximum amount of information to be retrieved about the identity of the deceased – and the causes and circumstances of that person's death – forensic archaelogists have the most experience to perform such a task. Many of the archaeologists who specialize in this field of investigative and legal archaeology have a background in some aspect of biology, such as molecular genetics or taphonomy (the chemical and biological processes that take place when materials decay).

The techniques that these archaeologists use at a crime scene are no different to those they would use to excavate human remains in an archaeological context. What they bring to the forensic process is a detailed knowledge of how to excavate buried remains, what to look for and how to interpret the pattern of evidence found. Where once the police might have used basic techniques to excavate a grave, archaeologists have taught them how to be systematic and precise.

Forensic methods

Called in by the police or by human rights agencies to help locate graves, forensic archaeologists use aerial photography and satellite imagery to survey for disturbed ground that might, for example, be the site of a mass grave, and remote sensing techniques help to refine the area of search. Precise excavation of grave sites follows archaeological principles in labelling and recording precise find spots of objects in and around the grave, using grids and three-dimensional measuring equipment. Soil samples are collected for environmental evidence, such as pollen, plant remains, charcoal, snails and insects and ash, all of which can help a forensic archaeologist to say something about the environment a victim has been in prior to their burial.

Studying human skeletal remains can help determine the age, sex and height of the deceased, and various individual characteristics, including body mass, musculature, state of health and dental imprint, all of which can be matched against health records. These are used not only in murder investigations, but also victim identification following disasters, such as earthquakes, flooding, terrorist attacks, fires or plane accidents. In murder investigations and post mortems, the archaeologists' knowledge of pathology can help distinguish between older injuries, those that might have been the cause of death and those that the body suffered after death.

Forensic archaeologists also look for objects associated with the grave, for instance clothing and footwear,

Above Protective white suits must be worn by forensic archaeologists working at sensitive sites to prevent contamination of the evidence.

Left French forensic expert Pascal Kintz proved by the chemical analysis of his hair, shown here, that Napoléon died of arsenic poisoning.

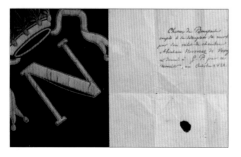

Above Some ancient burial sites can still be regarded as crime scenes. Archaeologists will inspect bones for injuries that reflect foul play.

Above Forensic techniques have established that Beethoven was killed by lead in the medicines he was prescribed.

documentation, weapons and other potential evidence. They use their knowledge of the chemical and biological processes involved in decay to explain how long the items might have been buried in the ground and look for the tell-tale evidence of fingerprints, blood, DNA or fibres that can help trace the body to a person or crime scene.

Clues in human hair

Forensic archaeology has been used successfully on numerous occasions to try to identify the cause of death of various historical figures, often based on an analysis of the chemical residues in human hair. By studying both hair and bone fragments, the Viennese forensic expert Christian Reiter was able to determine, for example, that Beethoven's death in 1827 at the age of 57 was caused by lead poisoning. The exposure to lead probably came from treatments that Beethoven was given by his physician, Dr Andreas Wawruch, for cirrhosis of the liver, which was given as his cause of death at the time. Dr Wawruch's diary reveals that he prescribed salts containing lead, and that he rubbed cream containing lead into Beethoven's abdomen.

Professor Martin Warren, a forensic scientist of the University of Kent in England, studied a lock of hair from King George III, which had been kept at the Science Museum in London since the king's death in 1820. He concluded that the king had also taken medication that caused death, rather than cured him. Late in his life, the king had severe attacks of the hereditary illness called porphyria, and was treated with an 'emetic tartar' made from antimony, which contains high levels of arsenic.

In the case of Napoléon Bonaparte, arsenic poisoning was long suspected as the cause of the fallen French emperor's death in 1821, partly because Napoleon's body was found to be remarkably well preserved when it was moved in 1840, and arsenic is a strong preservative. Arsenic levels were indeed found in locks of Napoleon's hair. Some scientists have theorized that he was deliberately poisoned, while others thought his hair tonic contained arsenic, or that it came from the copper-arsenic minerals in the green wallpaper in his room. Now it is thought more likely that it came from antimony potassium tartrate given as a purgative to Napoléon in an attempt to cure stomach cancer, the real cause of his death.

Jack the Ripper

Ian Findlay, Professor of Molecular and Forensic Diagnostics at the University of Brisbane, has concluded that Jack the Ripper, the notorious serial killer who killed at least five women in London, England, in 1888, but who was never caught, could have been a woman. His conclusions came from extracting DNA from the gum on the envelopes and postage stamps of letters sent by 'the Ripper' to the police. They confirm the suspicions of Frederick Aberline, the detective who led the investigation at the time. The prime suspect is Mary Pearcey, who used a similar modus operandi to the Ripper in murdering her lover's wife, and who was hanged for that offence in 1890.

Finding out more

A number of colleges offer courses in forensic archaeology.
• Mercyhurst Archaeological Institute, Erie, Pennsylvania: mai.mercyhurst.edu – website has links to numerous related resources
• The Institute of Archaeology and Antiquity, Birmingham, UK: www.arch-ant.bham.ac.uk/arch/pforensic.htm
• The School of Conservation Sciences at the University of Bournemouth, UK: www.bournemouth.ac.uk/conservation

Above Historic crimes might yet be resolved using forensics: Jack the Ripper's knife is now displayed at London's Police Crime Museum.

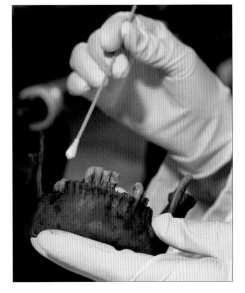

Above Forensic examination of jawbones and other body parts has enabled archaeologists to determine the ages of many victims of Pompeii.

A Face from the Past

One of the skills used in forensic archaeology is the reconstruction of someone's appearance from their skeletal remains. The techniques involved in bringing faces back to life can also be used to visualize historic figures, such as Helen of Troy and Cleopatra.

Above An archaeologist restores a painted wooden sarcophagus found near the famous Step Pyramid in Saqqara, Egypt.

Using anatomical knowledge and computer modelling mixed with the skills of a trained artist and portrait painter, a specialist in facial reconstruction can sculpt the head of a 2,000-year-old Roman soldier, a 1,500-year-old Anglo-Saxon farmer or even a 25,000-year-old Neanderthal.

The same skills have been used to reconstruct famous faces from the past. Shakespeare, Columbus, Cleopatra and Helen of Troy have all been visualized in this way, although in all four cases their reconstructions are based on portraits from coins, paintings, tomb sculptures, painted vases, written descriptions or pure guesswork, rather than on skeletal evidence. Much has been made of the fact that Cleopatra was not conventionally beautiful by modern Western standards, judging by the portraits on her coinage, a fact confirmed by the Roman author Plutarch, who said of Cleopatra that 'her actual beauty was not in itself so remarkable', instead the appeal lay in 'the attraction of her person, joining with the charm of her conversation, and the character that attended all she said or did…it was a pleasure merely to hear the sound of her voice'.

Archaeology has yet to find a way of recovering Cleopatra's voice, but where a skull survives as the basis for facial reconstruction, archaeologists no longer have to imagine or fantasize. Reconstructions are based on relating the distinctive clues provided by the human skull – jaw size, brow shape, nose profile – to the soft tissue that might have formed the living face. Such craniofacial reconstructions are based on a large body of measurements and other data relating to the musculature of the human face and how this varies according to a person's diet, age, gender and race. However, there is still much that is speculative, because the precise appearance of noses and ears is impossible to predict from skull shape, and these add substantially to the unique appearance of the individual.

Kremlin beauties

Using such techniques, Sergie Nikitin, one of Russia's leading forensic archaeologists, has reconstructed the facial appearances of several of Russia's tsarinas and princesses from the 15th to the 18th centuries. Their remains come from Moscow's Kremlin cemetery, used for the burial of tsars and their families from 1407 to 1731. It was destroyed by Stalin in the 1930s as part of his campaign to break the influence of the Church in Russia. However, encased in stone coffins, the remains of five women, including those of Marfa Sobakina, the third wife of Ivan the Terrible, survived. Marfa was chosen by Ivan from 1,500 potential wives, chosen as the most beautiful women of their day. Their beauty may have been their downfall, as Marfa died two weeks after her marriage – poisoned, it is said, by a jealous rival, but more likely killed by use of toxic cosmetics based on white lead, mercury and arsenic.

The face of Tutankhamun

Putting a real face on the past is such an important technique for engaging the public that large sums have been invested in projects to accompany blockbuster exhibitions. One example

Above The face of Helen of Troy, as sculpted by the Neoclassical artist Antonio Canova.

Above The golden mask of Tutankhamun concealed the boy pharaoh's face for decades.

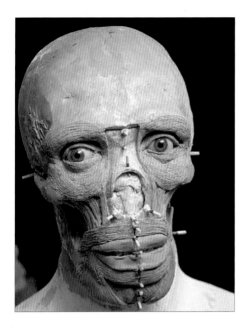

Above The partially reconstructed face of a Neanderthal woman who lived some 35,000 years ago near Sainte-Cesaire, France.

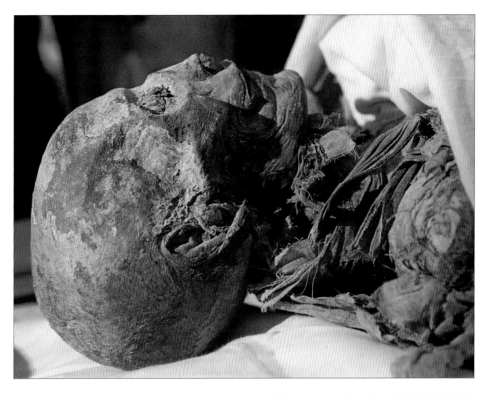

Above Queen Hatshepsut was among the most powerful female monarchs of ancient Egypt. She declared herself pharaoh after the death of her husband-brother Tuthmosis II.

was the reconstruction of the appearance of Tutankhamun, whose tomb has been the subject of enormous public interest since its discovery by Howard Carter in 1922.

The beautiful golden death mask of the boy pharaoh (who ruled from 1333–1324BC) has become an instantly recognizable icon for ancient Egypt, but three teams of scientists – Egyptian, French and American – used a battery of scientific techniques in 2005 to see what Tutankhamun really looked like and to find out as much as possible about his life from his mummified remains.

In reconstructing Tutankhamun's appearance, the three teams worked separately, and from different evidence. The Egyptian team worked from three-dimensional scans of the pharaoh's skull, while the French and American teams worked from casts of the skull; the American team worked blind, with no idea of whose appearance they were reconstructing. The resulting consensus was shown as the front cover of the June 2005 edition of *National Geographic* magazine, and caused some controversy because of the selection of a medium skin tone and hazel coloured eyes, illustrating the limits of current science in

determining the precise appearance of genetically inherited characteristics that are difficult to determine from the skull alone.

An untimely death

One theory about the boy's death – that he died from a murderous blow to the head – was discounted through the discovery that loose pieces of bone at the back of the skull were removed as part of the embalming process and did not represent a mortal wound. However, a fractured leg bone – previously dismissed as the result of rough handling by embalmers after death, is now thought to have been caused by a fall from a height during the boy's short life; he also has some missing ribs that were sawn off, archaeologists believe, in an attempt to save the Pharaoh's life. It now looks as if Tutankhamun met his death in a riding or hunting accident, perhaps falling of his horse, resulting in the broken leg, and a kick to the chest that broke his ribs. Such severe injuries, if turning gangrenous, might have killed the young king within hours.

Revealing the boy king

The preserved face – and feet – of a boy king was revealed to the public for the first time in roughly 3,000 years when, in November 2007, the mummy was removed from its golden tomb and the linen covering his skin was removed by archaeologists. The mummy was later placed in a sealed cabinet within the tomb to protect it from the detrimental effects of exposure to humidity and warmth that began with Carter's famous exposition.

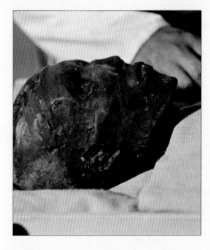

Above At last, the unmasked face of Tutankhamun is revealed to the world.

Battlefield Archaeology

As an important component of the world's cultural heritage, battlefields have increasingly become subject to the scrutiny of specialist archaeologists, whose twin aims are to commemorate and honour the war dead and to understand better some of the events on which history has turned.

Above A rare World War II 'Alan Williams Turret', designed for machine gun fire and installed to protect airfields.

The story of how battlefield archaeology has developed from a niche interest into a mainstream specialism in such a short time mirrors many other developments in archaeology and society. In its early days, archaeology was often run by military personnel, including Lieutenant-Colonel Thomas Edward Lawrence – perhaps better known as Lawrence of Arabia. His survey of the Negev Desert in 1914, funded by the Palestine Exploration Fund, served the dual purposes of archaeological and military intelligence. Another example is the work of Brigadier Sir Robert Eric Mortimer Wheeler, who ran his digs like a military operation and interpreted the classic sites that he dug – such as Maiden Castle – as massive prehistoric fortifications. Trained in the classics, fed on a literary diet of Greek and Roman war and heroism and with personal experience of two world wars, it was not surprising that archaeologists of the first half of the 20th century often exaggerated the role of armed and organized conflict in the rise and fall of civilizations.

However, by the second half of the 20th century, and with growing momentum in the 1960s and 1970s, the reaction to war (coinciding as it did with anti-Vietnam demonstrations) led many archaeologists to seek alternative explanations for cultural change. Mortimer Wheeler's Maiden Castle, along with 'hill forts' in general, became market places and ritual sites rather than battlefields, and major developments in art and industry, in architecture and agriculture, were seen as the products of peace, not war, of trade and consumerism, not the imposition of a lifestyle by conquerors on the conquered.

Ancient violence

From these extreme positions, a middle way is now being sought. The precise extent to which warfare and violence played a part in changing the course of history is a topic that will always be debated by archaeologists, but that debate is increasingly informed by the study of ancient skeletal remains to find injuries that can best be explained as war wounds or evidence for human violence. Recent studies have shown that a surprising number of prehistoric skeletons do bear fractures or cuts that look like the results of lethal violence. The puzzle is whether this represents some form of routine warfare – the constant struggle of one community set against another – or

Above The multiple ramparts of Europe's largest Iron-Age hillfort at Maiden Castle, Dorset, UK, built 450–300BC.

Above Archaeologists survey underground tunnels built for storing precious works of art and top secret documents during World War II.

Above Archaeologists used GPS (Global Positioning Systems) to pinpoint the location of artefacts found on the site of Little Bighorn.

The Battle of Little Bighorn

Further back in time, the historical record might be less rich, or may not exist at all. A pioneering example of battlefield archaeology was the study of the site of the Battle of Little Bighorn on 25 June 1876, when Lt Col George A. Custer and 263 US army soldiers met their deaths in battle with several thousand Lakota Sioux, Cheyenne and Arapaho warriors. Here, metal-detector survey was used to locate and map discarded weapons and ammunition. Excavators discovered 320 historic artefacts connected with the battle, including arrow points, trouser buttons, boot nails, a screw from a Colt revolver backstrap and an assortment of cartridge cases and bullets. By careful analysis of these scant remains, it was possible to begin to construct a model of the placement and movement of people across the battlefield. Despite its mythic significance, almost nothing had been known previously about the precise details of this battle, commemorated in books and film as the site of 'Custer's Last Stand'. The evidence from the archaeology has now enabled a National Monument to be constructed telling the story of all those who took part in this conflict of two cultures.

Above A Colt .45 bullet located on the battlefield using metal detection.

Above Metal detectors survey the front line at Little Bighorn.

Above Locations of finds obtained via GPS were later added to a map of the battlefield.

whether we are seeing a rare event. It is perfectly possible that the remains that come from prehistoric burial mounds represent an elite warrior class, or they might even have been selected for burial in this way because of their heroism in, for example, a dual or a violent ritual.

Elusive battlefields

As well as studying human remains, archaeologists also study battle locations to understand precisely what happened in specific battles and to ensure that battlefields are recognized as important places for society as a whole. One of the first challenges facing battlefield archaeologists is to identify where the battle actually took place. Historically well-documented battles, such as the Battle of Bosworth Field (which led to the ascendancy of the Tudor dynasty on the English throne) or the Battle of Culloden, Bonnie Prince Charlie's attempt to regain the British throne) are surprisingly elusive when it comes to finding evidence on the ground.

Battlefields may only have witnessed events that lasted a mere three hours or so – perhaps a day at most – so there is far less evidence to find than with long-inhabited sites. Looters often searched battlefields after the event, so little survives other than the small items considered of little value. Typical tell-tale finds might consist of something as small as a button from a military uniform, a cap badge, or the remains of weapons and ammunition.

Battlefield archaeologists, therefore, expend a lot of time in field survey work, talking to farmers about any finds they might have made during ploughing and cultivation, looking at collections built up by metal detectorists, and studying the topography to try to match the landscape to historical descriptions of the battlefield.

Commemoration

The aim of this survey work is to locate as precisely as possible the location of historic battle sites, to compile battlefield inventories and to develop management and conservation plans to ensure that such historic places are well-protected from development and their significance is fully understood. Commemorating those who died becomes all the more important with recent battlefields, where archaeologists can identify the soldiers who died, and where there might be war veterans and relatives still alive who knew those men and women. Working on such sites is, in the memorable phrase of leading battlefield archaeologist, Nicholas Saunders, about 'excavating memories', where the emotional relationship between us and the past is far stronger than on most archaeological sites.

In the case of such large conflicts as the two world wars, battlefields can be discovered by accident, often as a result of a new road scheme or development. Battlefield archaeologists are called in to exercise skill and sensitivity in the excavation, recording and recovery of the remains, using historical resources, such as war records, diaries, letters, memoirs and photographs to write the detailed story of the site.

Ethnoarchaeology

From the Greek ethnos, *meaning 'race', ethno refers to a people or culture, thus, the term ethnoarchaeology. Specialists in this field immerse themselves in other people's lives — especially those of people whose way of life is more comparable to that of the prehistoric or medieval past than to modern life.*

Above Ancient lifestyles: canoes provide the main form of transport for Yanomami tribespeople in South America.

One of the most difficult challenges facing any archaeologist is to understand the meaning of artefacts and structures that survive in the archaeological record. To give one example, an archaeologist might be able to deduce that a certain type of pot, or a certain type of decoration, is associated with the dead because its type or decoration is found mainly on pots used in cemeteries and cremations, or from its absence in domestic contexts. However, this glimpse into the meaning of the pot is limited without a knowledge of why that shape or decoration is used in this way. 'If only we could go and ask the makers and users why they did this', is often the unspoken cry of many an archaeologist.

Ethnoarchaeology (also called social or cultural anthropology or ethnography) aims to do exactly that. Its practitioners live among the people of their chosen study group, aiming to integrate themselves to become as unobtrusive as possible, to learn their language and to devote a considerable period of their lives to asking questions and observing how people live.

The diversity of human experience

Perhaps one of the most celebrated of such studies was that of pioneer anthropologist Margaret Mead, whose book called *Coming of Age in Samoa* (1928) looked at the rites of passage associated with the transition from childhood to adulthood. The book was extremely influential in its time, but it was later criticized as being too naive and painting too idealistic a picture, taking too much on trust and not allowing for the fact that the people that she interviewed might not be telling the literal truth.

The methods used by ethnoarchaeologists have thus had to adapt to the fact that people might not want to divulge the detail of complex moral, religious and cosmological systems, so a new method of 'participant observation' was subsequently born in which the researcher gained a close and intimate familiarity with a given group of individuals through living with them over an extended period of time and observing at first-hand their interactions with their natural environment and such domestic and economic activities as food preparation, disposal of refuse and religion and ritual.

More recently, social anthropologists have realized that fundamental truths about human responses to their environments can be found anywhere. Walking down any street with an enquiring mind will suggest a hundred lines of anthropological enquiry about

Above Roma people have been gathering for centuries to honour their patron, Saint Sarah the Black, in the Camargue, southern France.

Left Proud of their roots, Native American Sioux continue to re-enact lost lifestyles in South Dakota, USA.

Above Observing tool use in pre-industrial societies provides valuable clues to the meaning of archaeological finds.

Objects and their meaning

To illustrate how objects can be containers of meaning, a professor once brought a plastic three-dimensional jigsaw puzzle of the globe into his lecture. He broke the jigsaw into its component parts and gave a piece to everyone in the room as he talked, as a souvenir of the lecture. If that piece of jigsaw became an archaeological find, the archaeologist would simply think 'jigsaw'. The archaeologist would not know that that jigsaw piece connected its owner to a specific lecture, on a particular day and at a particular place, and to a group of people who all shared the experience. Much of the material that is found in archaeology might have similar multiple resonances whose meanings can no longer be read without ingenuity and guesswork, and even then, archaeologists might never know what special meaning the object had for its owner.

the way that people behave and interact. Anthropologists today no longer work exclusively with the fast-disappearing groups of people who remain unaffected by modernity. Instead, they study all forms of human experience, including nomadic life-styles and sedentary, conformist and non-conformist.

In the case of ethnoarchaeologists, they specifically look for the way that material culture reflects the manner in which people express gender and ethnicity, race, religion, family life or kinship. They also study such diverse topics as military culture, gang culture, gay culture, tattoo culture, the role of the media in society and popular culture, and the impact of globaliz-ation, drug culture, punk culture, Romani culture, the culture of the Japanese 'salaryman' and of the 'geisha'.

Observation as a stranger

The aim for the archaeologist is to try to turn him- or herself into a 'someone from Mars', taking nothing for granted and constantly asking what this means, how the meanings are expressed and transmuted and what impact they have on those who share or reject these cultural phenomena. Attempts to codify the results into some sort of universal system of symbol and meaning led to the rise of structuralism in archaeology in the 1960s and 1970s, built on the desire to place the study of human culture on a scientific and systematic basis.

Above The lifestyles of the Veda people in Sri Lanka may differ little from those of our Mesolithic hunter-gatherer ancestors.

Structuralism itself borrowed heavily from Freudian psychology, and the idea that polarities – such as black/white, male/female, young/old, inside/outside, clean/dirty, living/dead, summer/winter and famine/plenty – are fundamental to the human psyche. Some practitioners also approached the topic with a Marxist perspective that saw history in terms of immutable processes connected with the control of economic resources, which many critics of such thinking said reduced human beings to agents within a system that was beyond their influence or control, denying their freedom to act on the basis of personal choice.

Multiple resonances

Practitioners today are still happy to generalize about the phenomena they observe, but they are no longer so dogmatic in asserting that all humans

Above Ethnoarchaeologists working with Romani people in Europe have recorded beliefs that reflect very ancient taboos and polarities.

will behave in certain ways under certain conditions, or that all forms of behaviour can be reduced to a set of binary oppositions. Instead, what ethnoarchaeologists now bring to the subject is an awareness of the sheer complexity of human thought and behaviour. Normally in science the rule of Ockham's razor is observed, which says 'always look for the simplest explanation'. In studying human beings, the opposite often applies. What is found in archaeology often hints at the profundity and diversity of human behaviour, as those who study shamanism and the mindset behind rock art and cave paintings will testify. Indeed, even trying to explain in objective terms what a cathedral, church, temple or mosque is all about will quickly dispel any notion that human behaviour can be reduced to simple formulae.

Linguistic Archaeology

Language is key to what distinguishes humans and apes, and like the human evolutionary tree, languages have a genetic history. One of the most fascinating areas of archaeology is the attempt to map that history, working back from today's languages to the origins of languages.

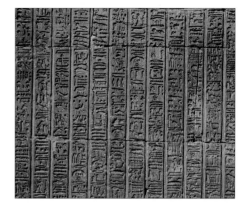

Above Stories in stone: hieroglyphs cover the walls of the ancient Egyptian temple of Kom Ombo (150BC).

Archaeologists who study human origins argue that it is language that makes us special. Our close relations in the evolutionary tree do not lack intelligence, but their intelligence is specific, based on a profound understanding of the local environment. The ability to think beyond that environment, to make an imaginary leap from the visible world to the worlds that lie beyond vision – whether over the physical horizon or in the supernatural world – are dependent on language, by which is meant not simply the association of a certain sound with a certain object, but a varied, fluid vocabulary, governed by rules of grammar.

Language probably developed as a consequence of social complexity. Primates in the wild live in relatively small groups, stay together and maintain regular physical and visual contact with all the other members of the group by sharing food and grooming. *Homo sapiens* developed language as a tactic for coping with the growth of the social group to the point where it is no longer feasible to know what is happening throughout the group. Like friends staying in touch via a telephone, language is key to sharing experiences that happen outside the immediate field of vision and for extending out knowledge of the world beyond localized understanding.

Songlines and Dreaming

The first language, if we could ever get back to it, might have a vocabulary related to geography and to the ability of people to be able to tell each other where they have been, and what they saw on, say, a hunting or foraging expedition. This is similar to the celebrated songlines, or dreaming tracks, of indigenous Australians, whose orally transmitted song cycles evoke the landscape as created during the primordial Dreaming, when the earth and everything upon it was created. These include such detailed descriptions of trees, rocks, waterholes and other landmarks that indigenous people can use them to navigate large distances through the deserts of Australia's interior.

It has been estimated that there were up to 750 distinct languages or dialects in Australia prior to the arrival of European colonists, and of these, some 200 indigenous languages survive today. How all these languages relate to each other is not at all clear, but attempts are being made to analyse and classify the languages in order to draw up a family tree for language groups and their influence on each other.

Indo-European linguistics

Such complex and difficult work goes back to the 18th century, when linguistic scholars began to recognize similarities in vocabulary between languages spoken in India and Europe. They theorized that people living in a swathe across Asia and Europe once spoke the same proto language – Indo-European – and that the linguistic

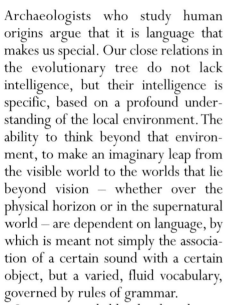

Above Some languages and writing systems are based on pictures or symbols, including ancient Egyptian, Chinese and Mayan scripts.

Above The evil spirit Nabulwinjbulwinj features in Aboriginal lore and in rock art at the Anbangbang rock shelter, Kakadu, Australia.

Above The Kharosthi alphabet, widely used in north-west India and central Asia until the 4th century AD, provides clues to even older Aramaic languages.

Above Languages as diverse as Spanish, Hindi, English and Urdu are ultimately derived from a common Indo-European tongue.

Above The Dead Sea Scrolls, displayed in Washington DC, are written in Aramaic, Greek and Hebrew, and are among the only surviving original texts of the Bible.

diversity we now experience is the result of communities developing new vocabularies in isolation, just as the many languages of modern Europe have evolved from Latin.

A purely theoretical language, the Proto-Indo-European language (PIE) was constructed by linguistic archaeologists by looking for words that are common to the modern languages derived from Indo-European, including Spanish, English, Hindi, Iranian, Bengali, Russian, German, French, Italian, Punjabi and Urdu. There are thousands of root words, including many of the words we use for counting and words indicative of a pre-industrial lifestyle, such as sheep, dog, wolf, fire, horse, cow, wife, king, priest, weave and wheel.

Links between languages and archaeology

More recently, linguistic archaeologists have observed that there is a strong correlation between language and genes. In very simple terms, people who speak the same language also share the same distinctive genetic profile. This discovery has revolutionized the study of language evolution, because genetic scientists are able to give approximate dates to the evolution of specific gene types (known as haplotypes), which in turn helps to give a relative date for the language. Linguistic historians can now see which people and languages in Africa, for example, are related and identify the linguistic characteristics that they share and that might provide clues to the common language they once spoke.

It might be argued that language is not archaeology because it is not material, but language overlaps in many ways with some of archaeology's central concerns, such as the migration of people, the creation of cultural identity (what is more distinctive of a culture than its language?) and the influence of one culture over another (demonstrated by the absorption of new words from one language into another). Linguistic theorists imagine that there are several different ways that languages change and evolve, all of which have archaeological implications. They can affect each other simply through regular contact, by elite dominance, where one group imposes its language on another, or bars access to wealth to those who don't speak the language, or through some form of innovation (such as pottery, metallurgy or farming) that has its own vocabulary, relating to technological practice.

Although the study of linguistic history goes back to the 18th century, it is, in its latest manifestation, still in its infancy, with many questions still to be answered by geneticists, linguists and archaeologists working together.

Basque

Euskara, the language of the Basque people of north-west Spain, has been identified as a relic of a language older than Indo-European, just as DNA studies have identified the Basque people as having a distinctive genetic profile. Numerous attempts have been made to explain why Euskara has become what is known as a 'language isolate' (meaning that it is not derived from nor related to any other language), including the possibility that the Basque people are the remnants of an early migration of people into Europe who survived the ice ages that led to the demise of other early European settlers.

Archaeoastronomy

Many of the world's archaeological monuments incorporate significant alignments that relate to the movements of the sun, moon, planets, constellations and stars. Students of archaeoastronomy devote themselves to understanding what significance these alignments might have.

The 1965 publication of *Stonehenge Decoded*, in which astronomer Dr Gerald S. Hawkins argued that the monument was built to observe lunar and solar events, made a major new contribution to the understanding of the monument. It was followed by *Megalithic Sites in Britain* (1967) by Alexander Thom, Professor of Engineering at Oxford University, whose study of megalithic sites gave evidence for widespread astronomical knowledge in Neolithic Europe.

Simultaneously, research in the Americas established that the planting of crops and the distribution of water, in some of the major civilizations of pre-Columbian Central America, was controlled by a sophisticated calendrical system in which rocks and hilltops were used as markers for charting the passage of the sun and the seasons. Suddenly, it became possible to read whole landscapes, and not just isolated monuments, as evidence of a sophisticated understanding on the part of our ancestors of cosmic events and their impact on human life.

Lunatic fringe

Ironically, these early studies, although based on meticulous measurements and observations at many hundreds of sites, received a cold welcome among many traditional archaeologists, while being embraced enthusiastically by hippies, pagans and new-age groups seeking to recover pre-Christian wisdom, beliefs and religious practices. Ordinary archaeologists were deterred from engaging with this new evidence because it involved a detailed knowledge of advanced mathematics and astronomy – but evidence continued to grow and it led to the creation of the entirely new (and still thriving) discipline of archaeoastronomy.

One of the main activities of archaeoastronomers is the study of alignments, but they also study objects such as the

Above Many archaeologists now believe that the siting of ancient monuments and megaliths in Europe show ancient astronomical learning.

Nebra sky disc (*see* Metal Detecting) that might have an astronomical significance. Wary of the connection with pseudoscience and 'false' archaeology, many of today's academic archaeoastronomers are concerned with distinguishing between demonstrable facts and coincidences, and the starting point for such studies is the attempt to recreate ancient sky conditions, so that the data from alignment studies can be set in its correct astronomical context.

Some argue that early forays into the discipline were over-enthusiastic and attributed to the builders of stone circles and alignments a knowledge of astronomy that they did not really

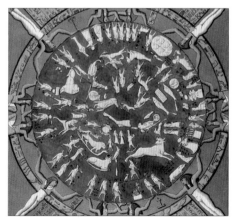

Above Ancient Egyptian people saw the stars forming the shapes of gods in human and animal form.

Left Druids gather at the ancient Neolithic site of Stonehenge, Wiltshire, England, to celebrate the summer solstice.

Above Prehistoric astrological art at Painted Rocks State Park, Arizona. Three points of sunlight cross the panel at the winter solstice.

Right The traditional Inca observations at Cusco continue to this day.

possess. Sophisticated patterns and alignments might simply be inherent properties of certain geometric shapes, rather than planned and conscious markers. Many east to west alignments are simple, and say nothing about the builders than that they wanted to express a sense of connection with the sun, the seasonal cycle, life, death, the ancestors, birth, renewal and fertility – simple connections that don't require deep astronomical knowledge.

Yet, there are real, discernible alignments that are common to many Mesolithic and Neolithic monuments throughout Europe, from the Urals to the west of Ireland and from Orkney to southern Spain. The big question about all these alignments is whether they mark sunrise or sunset, moonrise or moonset, summer or winter solstice. Answering such questions depends in part on other branches of archaeology, not least the study of animal remains from the feasting that took place at these monuments. In the case of Stonehenge, the age of the pig bones points to a winter festival, so the people who turn up at Stonehenge at the solstice (21 June) each year to watch the midsummer sunrise are celebrating a different event from that for which this and many similar monuments were intended – they should be turning up for the winter solstice sunset on 21 December.

New World evidence

In the Old World, archaeoastronomers have to base their investigations on mathematics and statistics. In the New World, they can consult the historical records of early colonizers, such as the 16th-century Spanish missionaries who lived among the people of Central and South America and wrote chronicles that today provide information about calendrical rituals. In August 1570, for example, the chronicler Cristóbal da Molina observed the Situa ritual at Cusco, the capital of the Inca Empire, in Peru, when, at the full moon, 4 groups of 100 warriors ran out of the palace along the kingdom's 4 main roads, aligned on the cardinal points of the compass, ordering everyone in the kingdom to wash their clothes, their tools and weapons in the rivers as a symbolic purification of the whole state.

Some ancient Inca practices survive today. Ethnographers in Peru often record conversations with farmers who still follow an agricultural cycle based on the Inca calendrical system, which uses the lunar cycle matched to the movements of the Pleiades constellation to guide their planting, irrigation and harvesting. It is this combination of practicality – the use of the natural cyclical events as a guide for agricultural activity – and the fascination with the sky and its capacity to fill people with awe, that makes archaeoastronomy an engrossing discipline.

Astronomy and power

Knowledge of the sun's movements can be translated into powerful political and ideological statements, as is explicit in Inca astronomical practices. These were linked to the political operations of the Inca king, who considered himself an offspring of the sun. Inca practice has its roots in much older monuments and religious beliefs: the 13 towers of Chankillo, built in the 4th century BC in the Casma-Sechin River basin, 150km (240 miles) north of Lima in Peru, is one of the oldest observatories for tracking the rising and setting of the sun yet found in South America. It is the equivalent of Stonehenge and hundreds of similar henges, enclosures, stone rows and earthen banks, passage graves, and megaliths built all over Europe during the Neolithic period.

Above The 13 towers of the solar observatory at Chankillo, Peru.

Case Study: Recreating Pugin's House

The Grange, the home of the 19th-century architect Augustus Pugin, set the pattern for neo-Gothic domestic architecture in Great Britain and abroad. Understanding the house and recreating its original appearance provides an excellent example of buildings archaeology in practice.

Above The striking wall covering with the Pugin family motto: *En Avant* ('Forward').

The Grange, located in the Kent town of Ramsgate in south-east England, was rescued from redevelopment in 1997 by the Landmark Trust, a charity that specializes in the restoration of historic buildings, which are then rented out as holiday homes. The Trust is selective in what it restores, but recognized in the sorry remains of a once-proud building a house of immense importance in the history of domestic architecture. It was designed by one of the most influential architects and designers of the 19th century, Augustus Welby Northmore Pugin (1812–52), a devout Catholic who did more than anyone to create the internationally ubiquitous Gothic revival, or Neo-Gothic style.

Pugin built many churches, schools, monasteries, convents and country houses, but he is best known as the man who designed the richly furnished interiors of the Houses of Parliament in London, after its medieval predecessor burned down in 1834.

Pugin built few domestic houses, but the house he built for himself in Ramsgate is particularly important because it set the template for much Victorian suburban architecture, not only in Great Britain but from Australia to the west coast of the United States. Restoring the house was an exercise in rediscovering the origins of the English middle-class suburban home.

Back to the original

Many changes had taken place since The Grange was completed in 1844, including various extensions and changes to the internal layout. Archive research enabled the Landmark Trust to locate notebooks and sketches that Pugin made of the original layout of the house. The floorplan has now been reinstated as Pugin intended, oriented to make the most of views of the sea, with three principal ground floor rooms – the drawing room, library and dining room – grouped around a square entrance hall, and a corridor leading off to the kitchen, to a square tower from which Pugin would watch passing ships, and to a private chapel.

If his design seems familiar now, it was radical in its time because it abandoned the classical symmetry of the preceding Georgian and Regency age. Sketches show that the house was designed from the inside out. Pugin thought first about what rooms he wanted and for what purpose, which ones needed fireplaces and which ones

Above Restoring the grand arch in the library using traditional craft techniques.

Left The exterior of the restored Grange. Pugin broke the architectural rules of his day by introducing asymmetry in place of the rigid symmetry of the Regency era.

needed windows, and he let the resulting plan dictate the external appearance. This was the reverse of the practice of the time, in which rooms were placed either side of a central passage, and life adapted to the spaces, rather than the other way around. 'Convenience', was one of Pugin's mantras when it came to domestic design and the asymmetry that resulted has since become the hallmark of English domestic architecture based on the central tenet that 'form should follow function'.

Rich interiors

Recreating the richly wallpapered, painted and panelled interior, furnished with pieces reflecting Pugin's own designs, as well as paintings and objects similar to those that had inspired his work was a bigger challenge. Archaeology came to the rescue here because, despite constant redecoration by subsequent owners, small traces of the original décor remained concealed beneath later work. Pugin also left behind a great deal of documentary evidence, including his own watercolour paintings of some of the rooms.

The covered porch was added by Pugin's son Edward, and opens into a generous hall, where Pugin kept a chest of clothes to give as charity to any beggar who came calling. The hall panelling is of the same simple joinery as was used throughout the house, above which the walls are papered with a red and green pattern based on the words of his family motto – *En Avant*, meaning 'Forward'. The striking diagonal design of the banisters was probably inspired by timber framing in northern France, which Pugin visited often, and the tiles on the floor incorporate Pugun's initials, AWP and family emblem, the black martlet (a heraldic bird, like a swallow).

Living rooms

The appearance of the library – one of the most important rooms in the house, because it was here that Pugin designed the interiors of The House of Lords – had to be recreated from shadowy marks on the walls and floorboards and from clues given in letters that Pugin wrote describing his working habits. These enabled the positions to be worked out of Pugin's desk, his bookshelves and his drawing

chests, as well as the wording of the text friezes that ran around the shelves, consisting of inspiring quotations from the Old Testament Book of Proverbs. The main cornice frieze also bore the names of Pugin's favourite people – saints, friends and clients – and places, designed to inspire him in his work.

In the dining room, original panelling survived that held a clue to the rest of the house, and it was possible to strip layers of paint to recover the original mahogany colour. The medieval look of the room was recreated from documentary as well as physical evidence, the ceiling being stencilled with a design based again on Pugin's initials.

Another Puginesque innovation that we take for granted today was the use of the kitchen for meals – Pugin designed the kitchen to be bright and airy, rather than an inferior room for servants, with large windows framing views of the neighbouring church. Fortunately, the original dresser had survived from the 1840s – the only piece of original furniture in the house.

Below The Grange dining room had its original panelling, but this had to be stripped of its later paint.

Above The restored study, with Pugin's desk and chair in place, and the onrnate frieze that encircled the room with biblical quotations.

Above The restored hallway and stairs have floor tiles and red and green wallpaper with Pugin's martlet (heraldic bird) emblem.

Above The restored dining room as Pugin would have known it when entertaining his London friends.

PUBLIC ARCHAEOLOGY

This final chapter looks at the work of archaeologists who specialize in the management and protection of the heritage, and who strive to engage the public in archaeology through many forms of advocacy, including policy research, political lobbying, educational work and journalism. Their work is rooted in questions about who owns the heritage – whether it is a universal resource that belongs to all humanity or it belongs to the person who owns the land on which potentially valuable objects are found.

If, as most archaeologists agree, archaeology is carried out in the public interest, it follows that archaeology should be rooted in public involvement – at the least, archaeologists have a duty to explain their work, and at best, archaeology should be a community activity. So here are some suggestions for ways that you can get involved in research, fieldwork and digging, and in more formal and structured learning about archaeology.

Opposite TV and podcast archaeology is now regularly broadcast to satisfy public demand.

Above Volunteers at a summer archaeology school practise the meticulous cleaning of sites during excavation.

Above Re-enactment has strong links to ethnoarchaeology: here we see the dress of 17th-century Jamestown, Virginia, USA.

Above Families visiting a heritage site are taught how to perfect their observation skills through drawing what they can see.

Conservation and Research

The idea that heritage belongs to everyone has led to the establishment of different schemes for identifying, protecting and conserving the best of the past. This involves achieving an effective balance between what archaeologists preserve and what is allowed to be developed.

Above Restoration of the burned Brittany parliament, France.

Since the mid-19th century, when writers and thinkers such as John Ruskin and William Morris began to argue for the protection of the best buildings from the past, many books have been written on conservation philosophy, many of which argue that governments worldwide need to take better care of the heritage, to put more money into archaeological conservation and research, and to frame policies that protect archaeology. In reality, this is far from easy. Archaeology is everywhere and to protect it all would be, to use a phrase favoured by the opponents of conservation, 'to preserve everything in aspic'.

Conservation also sits ill with the idea that private owners have the right to do whatever they like with their land and property. In reality, that is not true, and we all accept restrictions on our rights in the interests of a greater good – such as agreeing to obey traffic laws to prevent chaos on the roads. Heritage laws have been framed in many parts of the world that seek to balance the short term interests of private owners with the wider public interest in a heritage that belongs to the nation (or the human race) as a whole, and is worthy of protection for future generations.

A finite resource

The sheer volume of the material left by the some of the world's classical civilizations means that many people are faced by the remains of the past every day. Farmers in parts of Turkey,

Iran and Iraq describe their lands as 'pottery fields', because of the sheer amount of ancient material they turn up with their ploughs, and digging the garden in any city or town that was founded by the ancient Romans is likely to turn up pottery, tile, brick and nails from 2,000 years ago.

With such abundance, it is easy to be complacent, but archaeologists have realized over the last century that the survival of this rich legacy cannot be guaranteed. It is under threat from many forces, including looting and the effects of conflicts in areas such as Iraq, Afghanistan, Ethiopia and Nepal, to name just a few. In other places neglect is the problem: in Italy, Greece, north Africa and Turkey there is so much archaeology that governments cannot fund its conservation, or guard it against theft or damage.

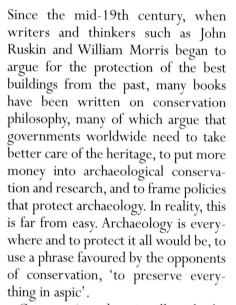

Above Centuries-old agricultural methods in Turkey are better for preserving buried archaeology than modern farming techniques.

Even in countries where war and looting are not endemic, construction projects or simple changes in agricultural practice can destroy precious archaeology. This occurred in Great Britain, for example, when cattle farmers devastated by foot and mouth disease, ploughed up pasture to grow potatoes. In the process they eradicated thousands of years of buried archaeology. Another example is when big office developments in the City of London involved the excavation of large holes that contained the record of the city's history.

Above Some excavation sites host tours to encourage visitors to learn about the historic treasures hidden beneath their city streets.

Left World Heritage status helps protect these 7th-century Buddhist carvings at the Longmen Caves, Henan province, China.

Above Medieval Tallinn, capital of Estonia, has survived numerous wars to become a World Heritage Site in 1997.

Monument protection

In response to such threats, archaeologists have long aspired to creating comprehensive lists of archaeological sites – and that term includes standing buildings, historic landscapes, gardens and battlefields, as well as buried archaeology – so that they can be fenced and protected from development. In some countries and states (but by no means all), these lists serve as the basis for legislation to protect heritage at every level, from internationally important sites to local heritage.

At the bottom of the pyramid are conservation areas, districts within cities, towns and villages where owners are encouraged to maintain the historic character of their properties and must apply for permission for alterations or extensions that might then have to be carried out using traditional materials – timber windows, rather than plastic, or stone walls and roof tiles instead of concrete. At the next level are sites that are regarded as nationally important, and that are protected from all forms of development, being conserved as prime examples of historic property. Then there are conventions that are regional in scope and that aim to protect not just buildings and buried archaeology, but whole landscapes. These are often protected by being

The origins of monument protection

The very first archaeological inventories date from the early 19th century in France, where the Comité Spécial des Arts et Monuments was set up in 1837 and charged with the task of drawing up a list of ruins and buildings worthy of state protection. Prosper Mérimée was appointed to the post of inspector-general of historical monuments, but he was sceptical of the enterprise, which he described as 'naive administrative romanticism'. He predicted that to catalogue all of France's archaeology would 'take 200 years and fill 900 volumes'. Mérimée was a pragmatist, and decided that the list of monuments to be protected should bear some relationship to the scale of the budget available for their conservation. He eventually produced a list of 59 monuments (the state allocated a mere 105,000 francs for their restoration).

designated as national parks – in the United States and Canada, national park status is the primary means by which outstanding natural and archaeological landscapes are conserved.

World Heritage Sites

At the apex of the pyramid are World Heritage Sites, designated by the World Heritage Committee of UNESCO (the United Nations Educational, Scientific and Cultural Organization); these consist of sites that are considered to have 'outstanding universal value'. The list currently includes 830 sites, in 138 countries, ranging from well-known heritage icons, such as the Taj Mahal, Angkor Wat, Chichén Itzá and the Egyptian pyramids, to transnational sites such as the Frontiers of the Roman Europe, which includes sites such as Hadrian's Wall and the Upper German-Raetian border wall that stretches from the Atlantic coast of northern Britain, through Europe to the Black Sea, and from there to the Red Sea and across North Africa back to the Atlantic coast.

The aim of the World Heritage Committee is to designate those sites that genuinely have resonance for all the people of the world. They should help to reinforce the idea of common humanity that underlies efforts toward world peace and multiracial harmony – an example of heritage having a value above and beyond the purely academic.

Getting Involved

Being passionate about their discipline, archaeologists want to share their interest. As a result, amateur involvement is warmly welcomed, and there are many doors through which one can enter if he or she wants to find out more.

Undoubtedly the best way to learn about archaeology is to take part in an excavation. Working for two weeks on a dig will introduce you to basic field techniques and let you decide whether two weeks of digging is more than enough for one lifetime or whether you want to devote the rest of your life to the discipline.

Field schools

There is no one single comprehensive source of information about archaeology field schools, a good place to start, however, is the Archaeological Fieldwork Opportunities Bulletin (www.archaeological.org/webinfo.php ?page=10015), published by the Archaeological Institute of America annually. This institution also has an online database of fieldwork projects in which volunteers can participate: www.archaeological.org/webinfo.php ?page=10016. In Great Britain, there is a web-based service on the site of the Council for British Archaeology: www.britarch.ac.uk/briefing/field.asp.

Many universities run field schools that are designed for training the students enrolled at that institution, but that often accept a small number of guest diggers. It is worth looking at the website of your nearest university,

Above Many archaeological summer schools are crying out for volunteers – and some may offer the opportunity to travel abroad.

going to the school's department of archaeology and seeing what might be available. For example, the Bristol University Field School (www.bris. ac.uk/archanth/fieldschools) offers opportunities to work in England, France and the Caribbean, on field survey, excavation and underwater archaeology. You must expect to pay to take part in any of these projects, and in return for a small weekly fee, you can expect basic accommodation (perhaps a camp site), training, and the occasional evening lecture or excursion to other sites in the area.

Training digs

There are also a limited number of organizations that run field schools undertaking important research almost staffed by paying volunteers (the usual ratio is one experienced archaeologist to two or three beginners). The standard of training on these courses is high, but they are also more expensive than university field schools. You can find out more by following the links on the About Archaeology website (http://archaeology.about.com) or by investing in a copy of the publication called *Archaeo-Volunteers: the World Guide to Archaeological and Heritage Volunteering* (greenvolunteers.com). Archaeological summer schools and training excavations in Europe are listed on the Archaeology in Europe website (www.archaeology.eu.com/ weblog/index.html), and the website

Below Dutch students excavate and record the medieval walls of Utrecht, in the Netherlands, looking for evidence of the city's buried Roman origins.

for the magazine *Current Archaeology* (www.ilovethepast.com) has useful feedback from people who have been on training excavations, telling you what to expect and providing reviews of the good and the not so good archaeological training experiences.

Alternatively, you can visit the website of the Earthwatch Institute (www.earthwatch.org), an international environmental charity that promotes the involvement of volunteers in fieldwork projects in all the sciences. The organization runs some 140 projects in over 50 countries, and some are suitable for families and children, with projects ranging from excavation in Peru, to cave art research in Europe, to the recording of historic buildings in Armenia.

Themed travel

Of course, if you prefer archaeology without the hard work, several excellent travel companies provide holidays based on archaeology, where participants are introduced to the subject by leading specialists who offer a privileged insight into the subject as they give guided tours and lectures. They often take you to places that are perhaps not normally accessible

Below A student learns to excavate and record the foundations of a prehistoric building on a training excavation.

to tourists. Andante Travels (www. andantetravels.co.uk) is one of the best specialist tour operators in this field, and is perhaps the only such company in the world that is owned and run by archaeologists. The American-based Archaeological Tours (www. archaeologicaltrs.com) offers a similar international programme of tours led by leading American scholars. Another firm, Ancient World Travel (www.ancient.co.uk) specializes in trips to archaeologically rich destinations led by people who have, in many cases, directed the excavations that you will visit. The company also organizes weekend conferences at which top archaeologists provide an introduction to the many different aspects of the world of archaeology.

National and local societies

Yet another way in which to become involved in archaeology is to join a national archaeological society, or one of the literally hundreds of local archaeological and historical societies that exists around the world. In Great Britain, there is a comprehensive list of local societies, which can be found on the website of the Council for British Archaeology (www.britarch.ac.uk/ info/socs.asp). You can search for organizations in other parts of the world by using the links on the Archaeology on the Net website (members.tripod.com/~archonnet/).

National, regional and international societies exist to promote the study of just about any archaeological topic you can dream up, from the archaeology of specific materials, such as glass or building materials to the big themes of prehistoric, Roman or medieval archaeology. By typing in the relevant words – for example, 'glass' and 'archaeology' and the county in which you live – a search engine should quickly enable you to locate relevant societies via the internet.

If you join a society, expect a lecture programme, newsletter and field trips. The best societies run their own research projects, which you can join and learn from. In time you might feel

Above As well as being intellectually challenging, archaeology is also great fun and a healthy and sociable outdoor activity.

confident about embarking on your own project, in which case society membership is a good way of finding a mentor. Just as importantly, you can use the society to tap into the archaeological network and find out what is going on in your field of interest. It is a network that anyone can join. Every day all over the world there are public lectures being delivered in museums, universities and society meetings that anyone can attend.

Papers in archaeological journals are increasingly accessible on the internet, and if the books and papers that academics produce are sometimes written in language that looks more like social science or linguistic philosophy, there are also many popular books written by knowledgeable academics that will serve as a way in to the more abstruse parts of the archaeological spectrum.

Learning More

If you want to take your interest in archaeology a step further, colleges and universities offer a great range of study opportunities. In addition, there are the opportunities for self-guided learning through books, specialist magazines, television programmes, lectures and websites.

Archaeologists are great enthusiasts for their discipline, and they often write books and articles or appear on television programmes to explain their discoveries. This means that there is no shortage of sources for formal and informal learning.

Formal learning

Many schools, colleges and universities provide evening classes and extra-mural courses, along with lifelong learning opportunities built around archaeology. In Great Britain, you can study for formal qualifications in GCSE and A Level archaeology (see the Council for British Archaeology website at: www.britarch.ac.uk/cba/factsht7.shtml), or you can buy the standard textbooks that support this subject and work through them on your own. *The Archaeology Coursebook*, by Jim Grant, Sam Gorin and Neil Fleming, is written by teachers and is packed with links to relevant websites, along with tasks and exercises for consolidating your learning. Another book is *Archaeology: an Introduction*, by Kevin Greene, which is used by many adult students and undergraduates as their basic primer.

At the time of writing, online learning is still under development as a way of learning about archaeology in your own time. Oxford University's Department of Continuing Education offers two online learning courses, in the 'Origins of Human Behaviour' and in 'Ritual and Religion in Prehistory', and further modules are being tested by organizations in Great Britain such as the Archaeology Training Forum (www.archaeologists.net/modules/icontent/index.php?page=41). In the United States, the Archaeological Institute of America also provides a website (www.archaeological.org/webinfo.php?page=10260). When they are fully developed, they will offer a step up from simply reading about the subject, with structured approaches to the subject and the opportunity to share ideas and develop critical arguments through online interaction with tutors and fellow students.

Degree study

Typically, if you choose to study archaeology at university, you can expect to spend the first year in learning about core concepts, basic techniques and the broad outlines of world archaeology. Often you will be expected to take part in fieldwork as an intergral part of the degree. In the second year, you might be able to select specialist topics from a range of modules and in the third year you

Above More formalized learning in Sudan, where univeristy students are being taught the techniques of drawing and analysing pottery.

Above Simply visiting ancient sites, like Rome's Colosseum, is a great way to learn.

might be encouraged to undertake a piece of original research, writing it up as a dissertation.

Archaeology provides an entry into many professions because it develops a good training in scientific method, team work and problem solving and clarity of thinking and expression. Those archaeology graduates who stay in the profession can study further to equip themselves to work in museums, education or fieldwork. Around 5 per cent of those who complete their archaeology degrees will go on to do post-graduate study for three years, during which time they will produce a thesis – a written piece of original research – while beginning to develop skills as a teacher and lecturer, enabling them to be qualified for junior lecturer posts and to begin to work their way up the academic ladder to the ultimate goal: the title of professor.

Above Archaeology at degree level offers students the chance to develop their skills in team building and problem solving.

Self learning

However, learning about archaeology need not be structured or academic. You can share in the sheer excitement of archaeological discovery in scores of less formal ways. One is to subscribe to one of the leading archaeology magazines that are written for non- specialists and that do an excellent job in reporting on the latest thinking, finds and projects in the subject. Magazines such as *Archaeology* (www.archaeology.org/), *Current Archaeology* and *Current World Archaeology* (www.archaeology.co.uk/) and *British Archaeology* (www.britarch.ac.uk/BA/ba.html) all publish part of their content on their websites, so you can browse before deciding whether or not to subscribe.

In addition, there are some excellent websites that aim to capture archaeological news stories from around the world and provide links to the source, or succinct summaries. You can easily keep up to date with all the latest discoveries and ideas by spending 15 minutes a day browsing the daily news pages of the Archaeological Institute of America (www.archaeology.org/online/news/index.html) or the Archaeologica website (www.archaeologica.org/), both of which have links to the newspapers and journals in which the stories originally appeared.

Above Archaeologists are often rewarded by finding objects, like this Viking hairpin, that provide direct contact with past people.

Above Excavating cremated bone with a spoon to ensure none gets lost.

Lectures

For live lectures, a good starting place is the local museum, where the curatorial staff often give free lectures, as do invited specialists. This is an often overlooked aspect of museum activity. National museums in particular offer outstanding lectures related to their special exhibitions, where you might be fortunate to hear the world expert on the subject give a free lunchtime lecture or lead a personal guided tour of the galleries.

Some archaeological organizations also use blogs and webcams to communicate with fellow enthusiasts so that you can follow the progress of excavations on a daily basis and share the way that interpretations often change as the dig develops. By this means, you can keep in daily contact with what is going on at key world archaeology sites such as Çatalhöyük (*see* Case study: Çatalhöyük) at www.catalhoyuk.com/ or Stonehenge (*see* *Complex Societies*) at www.shef.ac.uk/archaeology/research/stonehenge, or on the Archaeological Institute of America's interactive dig website: www.archaeology.org/interactive/index.html.

Television

There are plenty of television stations that will provide a programme about a specific project or a series covering archaeological themes, such as human origins, or cave art. One long-running British series that is also broadcast on cable channels in different parts of the world is 'Time Team', which is well worth watching because, unlike most

Above Sieving soil at the site of the first Russian-American fort, Kodiak Island, Alaska, USA.

televion archaeology, it shows you what archaeologists do and how they make deductions from what they find. 'Time Team' reflects the processes of archaeology, rather than just the discoveries that are the staple fare of the many archaeological shows that are broadcast regularly on cable television stations devoted to history.

Further reading

For the places where you are likely to find the very latest in archaeological research results, you can try reading the archaeological journals, such as *Antiquity* (antiquity.ac.uk/) and *World Archaeology* (www.tandf.co.uk/journals/rwar). If you feel ready for truly indepth material, you can also try reading the science-based periodicals such as *Science* (www.sciencemag.org/) or *Nature* (www.nature.com/index.html) – but be aware that these latter magazines can be heavily technical and difficult to understand without a grounding in the subject.

To obtain such a grounding, there are two outstanding books, both of which are encyclopaedic in scope and written with lucidity and a thorough knowledge of the subject: *The Human Past*, edited by Chris Scarre, and *Archaeology: Theories, Methods and Practice*, by Colin Renfrew and Paul Bahn. These two books contain comprehensive cross references to the more advanced specialist books on the many topics that they address, making them the ideal starting point for exploring the many different branches of the archaeological family tree.

Case Study: Jamestown/ Colonial Williamsburg

Jamestown and Colonial Williamsburg are nearby neighbours in the American state of Virginia, and together they exemplify all that is best in community archaeology and the presentation of the past to the public through living history re-enactment.

Above A reconstructive model of the Jamestown fort 'cottage'.

Jamestown (originally also called James Towne and Jamestowne) was the site of the first permanent British colony in North America. It was officially founded on 14 May 1607 and named after the reigning British monarch, James I (1603–25). The early colonists built their first settlement on site on an island in the James River for defensive purposes, however, this mosquito-ridden swampy outpost lacked good farming land and drinking water. The colonists eventually relocated their capital to higher ground a short distance away in 1699, building the

new town named Williamsburg (because by this time, it was William III (1689–1702) who was reigning on the British throne).

The members of the first colony included John Rolfe, whose experiments in growing tobacco led to the colony's eventual economic survival. He also married Pocahontas, daughter of Wahunsunacock, Chief of the Powhatan Confederacy, establishing a period of peace with Native Americans in the region.

By the 20th century, it was assumed that all archaeological evidence of that first historic colony had been lost to the scouring tides of the James River. In 1994, the Association for the Preservation of Virginia Antiquities

(APVA), the charity that now owns the site, set up a project called Jamestown Rediscovery to test this theory. Within days of beginning work, a team of volunteer archaeologists, under the direction of Project Director Bill Kelso, began to recover early colonial artefacts. In 1996, the team successfully located the site of the original settlement, which was within its original triangular palisade walls.

Below (Top) Newly cast lead shot as it emerged from a 17th-century mould, with the runner still attached.

Below (Bottom) The corroded remains of a Scottish 'snaphaunce' pistol, used for personal protection by one of Jamestown's early settlers.

Below This montage shows what the very first Jamestown homes and stockades might have looked like.

Living archaeology

Since then, thanks to the water-logged conditions of the ground at Jamestown, hundreds of thousands of artefacts have been recovered, including the remains of several houses and wells, and the graves of several of the early settlers. What makes this site so exceptional is the huge effort that has gone into involving visitors, enabling them to observe archaeologists in action and ask questions about the progress of research at the site.

The spectacular discoveries from the site include arms and armour, medical instruments, ceramics, tools, coins, trade items, clothing, musical instruments, games and food remains. They are displayed in a museum called 'the Archaearium', an unusual word that Bill Kelso has coined from the Greek *archeo* ('ancient') and the Latin *arium* ('place'). It consists of a glass building that covers parts of the site of the archaeological excavation, linking the history and the finds directly to the 'ancient place' where they were found. As well as reconstructing the appearance of the fort 400 years ago, digital technology is used to show visitors precisely where the objects

Below The excavation of a boiler jar, dated to 1610. Analysis of this precious find suggests that the first Jamestown settlers distilled their own alcohol, not only to drink, but also as a medical antiseptic and anaesthetic.

were recovered from the site, along with videos showing them being unearthed and conserved, thus involving those visitors who cannot take part in the dig with a sense of what it is like to be the archaeologist who makes the discovery.

The wider landscape

Historic Jamestown (the island itself) is now part of a wider historic landscape that takes in the port, fields, waterways and subsidiary settlements – such as Martin's Hundred and Henricus – built by the growing colony as it expanded along the banks of the James and York Rivers. Some of these sites have been excavated, while others remain to be excavated, protected from development by the designation of the whole area as the 'Historic Triangle'. This historic area is managed by the National Park Service and takes in the Colonial Williamsburg living history museum and Yorktown, where General Cornwallis surrendered to George Washington in 1781, ending the American Revolution, plus recreations of a Native American village and replicas of the sailing ships that brought the early colonists to America.

Colonial Williamsburg stands on the high ground between the James and York Rivers, where it was to evolve into the centre of government, education and culture for the colony of Virginia. Today, the clock has been turned back by the removal of buildings later than

1780 to create a living history museum that aims to be as authentic as possible with its recreations of colonial life and crafts. It literally meets the people and shares the life of the colony's 17th and 18th-century inhabitants.

Like archaeology in the wider world, which has grown to embrace the whole sweep of human history and experience, including the human tragedies of slavery, imprisonment and war, Colonial Williamsburg has responded to criticism that it neglected the role of African Americans in colonial life (in the 1950s, African Americans were allowed to visit Colonial Williamsburg only one day a week). New programmes have been added to explain slavery and present a more rounded picture of the people and the era.

Finding out more

Up to the minute accounts of work in progress at Jamestown can be found on the Historic Jamestown website, (www.historicjamestowne.org/index.php), and the whole story of Bill Kelso's quest for the site of the original colony is told in his book, *The Buried Truth*. For the people of Colonial Williamsburg, and details of conferences, educational activities and events, see the Colonial Williamsburg Foundation's website at www.history.org/.

Below A complete, if corroded, iron breastplate emerges from the now-dry moat surrounding the Jamestown fort.

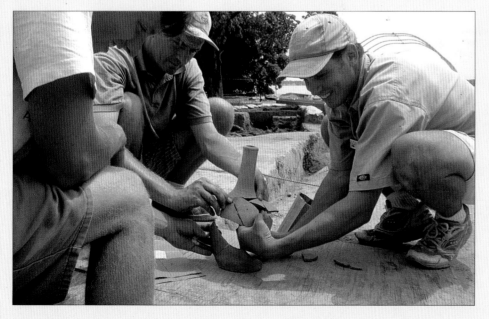

Index

Aberline, Frederick 103
Aegean Dendrochronology
    Project 50–51
Africa 19, 33, 46, 56, 60, 61, 65,
    66, 71, 84–85
    East Africa 56, 59, 62, 84
    North Africa 38, 39, 56,
        81, 118
    South Africa 56, 57, 59, 62, 65
agriculture 19, 70–71, 72–73, 80,
    86, 118
Aksumite Empire 85
Alexander the Great 82, 86
Algeria 65
America see Central America;
        North America; South
        America; United States
Americas, The 88–89
Amesbury Archer 37, 40
Angkor Wat 83, 86, 119
Anglo-Saxons 47
animal husbandry 70, 71
Apicius, De Re Coquinaria 43
Arabia 14
archaeoastronomy 112–113
archaeology 6–7
    getting involved 120–121
    post-excavation 9, 10–11
    studying 122–123
argon-argon dating 25
art 64–65
artefacts 14–15
Arthurian legend 39
Arun Estuary, Sussex 68, 69
Ashoka the Great 86, 87
Asia 19, 22, 38, 46, 51, 55, 61,
    62, 66, 72, 80, 86–87
assemblages 29
Assyria 78
Athens 39
Australia 22, 46, 59, 65, 66, 67
    human settlement 25, 63,
        70, 110
Australopithecines 57, 58, 59, 62
Austria 41
axes 15, 28, 76
Aztecs 78, 88

Babylonia 78, 79
Balkans 47, 73
Bantu expansion 84–85

Barbados 31
barrows 23
Basque 111
battlefield archaeology 106–107
Bayes, Thomas 23
Bayesian statistics 23
beads 28, 65
Beaker culture 78
Beethoven, Ludwig von 103
Benin Bronzes 36, 85
Bessemer, Henry 95
Bible 53, 66, 81, 111
boat-building 63, 65, 81, 84, 97
body art 65
bogs 69, 96
    bog offerings 36–37, 75
Bonaparte, Napoléon 102, 103
bones 43, 49, 53, 61, 62, 64
    animal bones 64
    DNA 49
Borneo 62
Bosworth Field 107
Boudicca 17, 25
box culverts 12
Breasted, Henry James 70–71
British Museum 77, 80
Brittany 73, 76, 77
bronze 15, 29, 36, 74, 76–77
Bronze Age 18, 28, 29, 54, 55,
    78, 79
    Flag Fen 74
    metalwork 33, 36, 37
    pottery 33, 39
bronze tools 54
brooches 29, 37
Brunel, Isambard Kingdom 95
Buddhism 82, 83, 86, 119
buildings 100–101
burials 45
butchery 63
Byzantium 14, 51

Cambridge University 49
camp fires 34, 62
Canada 21, 69
carbon-14 dating 18–19
Caribbean 31
Carter, Howard 84, 105
Carthage 78
carving 64
CAT scanning 6

Çatalhöyük, Turkey 90–91
caves 59, 62–63, 65, 84
Celts 39, 77
cemeteries 67
Central America 19, 34, 59, 71,
    81, 88–89, 112, 113
ceramics 10, 55, 83
Chad 56
Chankillo towers 113
Cheddar Man 46
Childe, Gordon 72, 73
China 36, 38, 45, 51, 61, 71, 78,
    80, 81, 86–87
Christianity 45, 82, 83, 85
    Tomb of Christ 99
chronological framework 12–13
chronologies 53, 54–55
Church 21, 83
churches 98–99
cities 80, 81, 86
civilizations 78–79, 80–81
Classical Age 82
clay pipes 27, 30, 83
Cleopatra 104
climate change 33, 34–35, 55,
    60, 62
clothes-making 64, 65
Clovis culture 23
coins 37, 55
    dating evidence 14, 15, 16
colonization 14
Columbus, Christopher 83
Confucius 86
Congo 60
conservation 49, 118–119
Constantine 82, 83, 99
Constantinople 39
copper 74
Copper Age 54, 55, 79
Corded Ware culture 74, 78
Cornwall, England 15, 47
Crete 14, 33, 72, 81
crop cultivation 70, 71
Cuba 36
Culloden 107
Custer, George 107
Cyprus 51
Cyrus the Great 86

Danube 27
Darby, Abraham I and III 94

Dart, Raymond 57
Darwin, Charles 54, 56
dating evidence 14–15
    earliest and latest dates 16–17
Dead Sea Scrolls 75, 111
dendrochronology 9, 24–25
    Aegean Dendrochronology
        Project 50–51
Denmark 54, 68, 75
diets 29, 42–43
    disease 44–45
digital data 48–49
digital reports 49
disease 44–45
    excavation 12–13
    matrices 12
DNA analysis 6, 46–47, 49, 56,
    57, 61, 87
    spread of agriculture 72–73
Doggerland 68
Douglass, Andrew Ellicott 24
drowned landscapes 62, 68–69

East Timor 63
Ecuador 80
Édessa, Greece 45
Egypt 14, 19, 40, 45, 51, 53, 71,
    78, 80, 81, 84, 104–105
El Chorro de Maíta, Cuba 36
England 60, 67, 68
environmental archaeologists
    32–33
Erik the Red 21
Ethiopia 57, 59, 85
ethnoarchaeology 108–109
Etruscans 37, 47, 55, 75, 81
Euphrates 12, 71, 80
Europe 55, 66
    agriculture 72, 73
    church building 15
    colonial expansion 14, 39, 71,
        83, 97
    dendrochronology 24
    early humans 64
    metalwork 36–37
    Neanderthals 22, 59, 61

Neolithic 23, 43
stone circles 45
European Route of Industrial
Heritage (ERIH) 95
evolution 56–57
excavation
digital data 48–49
ditches 12–13

farming *see* agriculture
Fertile Crescent 12, 70–71
Ficoroni Cist 55
field digs 120
Findlay, Ian 103
finds
classifying 26–27
fire making 58, 59
fishing 63, 65
Flag Fen, Peterborough 74
flint 29, 68
flooding 66–67
food preparation 40–41
footprints 69
Forbidden City, Beijing 37
forensic archaeology 102–103
forgeries 25, 83
founder crops 71
France 45, 60, 119
Friedrich, Walter 51

Gaza Strip 71
genetic information *see*
DNA analysis
Geographical Information Systems
see GIS
George III 101, 103
Georgia 60
Germany 25, 27, 68, 75
Ghana 62
Ghandi, Mahatma 95
Gilgal I, Jordan 71
Gilgamesh 66, 67, 81
GIS 49
glaciation 58, 66, 69, 70
globalization 83
Gnostic manuscripts 93
Gokcay, Metin 50
gold 15, 36, 74
grain crops 70, 71, 72
Grange, Ramsgate 114–115
grave goods 45, 67
Great Britain 37, 49, 67
genetic differences 47
Roman Britain 15, 17, 25,
42–43, 67

Greece 14, 39, 45, 47, 78, 81,
82, 83, 118
Aegean Dendrochronology
Project 50–51
Greenland 21, 51

Hadrian's Wall 42–43, 119
Harappa 80
Hawkins, Dr Gerald S. 112
henges 78
Herodotus 47, 53
Herschel, William 24
Hinduism 82, 83, 86
Holocene 66
Homer 53, 81, 82
hominids 22, 25, 46, 56, 57,
58–59, 60–61
Homo sapiens 33, 34, 35, 45, 58,
59, 61, 62, 65
world colonization 62–63
human origins 22, 33, 46, 53,
56–57, 58–59, 60–61
human remains
analysis 44–45
Hungary 73
hunter-gatherers 70, 72, 80, 88
hunting 64, 65
Huxley, Thomas 56
Hypocrates 42

Ice Maiden of Peru 89
Ice Maiden of Siberia 87
Iceland 21
Incas 32, 53, 78, 89, 113
India 60, 71, 80, 82, 86, 87
Indonesia 67
Indus Valley 80, 86
industrial archaeology 94–95
Industrial Revolution 94
Ingstad, Anne Stine 21
Ingstad, Helge 21
Institute of Nautical Archaeology
50
International Afar Research
Expedition 57
International Committee for
the Conservation of the
Industrial Heritage
(TICCIH) 95
intertidal archaeology 69
intrusive material 15
Iran 71, 118
Iraq 71, 79, 80, 81, 118
Ireland 73, 82
Iron Age 15, 54, 55, 76–77

metalwork 36, 37, 41
roundhouses 16, 74, 76
Islam 83
isotopes 43, 57
Israel 65, 69
Istanbul 50–51
Italy 37, 47, 50, 118
ivory 64

Janeism 82
Japan 38, 67, 71, 81
Java 62
Java Man 46, 57, 61
Jericho 19
jewellery 55, 74, 75
shells 64, 65
Jones, John Paul 97
Jordan 43, 60
Jürgensen, Christian 54

Kelso, Bill 124–125
Kenya 59, 60
kiln sites 39
Kintz, Pascal 102
Knossos 79, 81
Korea 71
Kostenski, Russia 64
Koster, Illinois 70
Kuhn, Steven L. 35
Kuniholm, Peter Ian 50

L'Anse aux Meadows, Canada 21
La Tène culture 36, 41, 77
landscape clearance 75
language 110–111
Lapita people 45, 81, 87
Lawrence, T. E. 106
Leakey, Louis 59
Leakey, Mary 59
Leakey, Richard 59
Lebanon 71
lectures 123
Libby, Willard Frank 19, 22
Libya 56
linguistic archaeology 110–111
Little Bighorn 106, 107
London 118
Great Fire 17
Lubbock, John 54
Lucy 25, 57

Macedonia 45, 78, 82, 86
Machu Picchu 53, 89
Mahudel, Nicholas 54
Malaysia 67

Manning, Stuart 50, 51
marine archaeology 96–97
Marxism 109
Mary Rose 96, 97
matrix 12–13
Mayans 31, 78, 81, 83, 88, 89
Mead, Margaret 108
measurement 81
medicine 42
Medicis 83
medieval times 15, 37
Mediterranean 12, 39, 66, 71, 73
Mérimée, Prosper 119
Mesoamericans 81, 88, 89
Mesolithic 49, 54, 66–67, 68, 69
Mesopotamia 66, 67, 79, 80, 81
metal detecting 15, 28, 37, 107
metal tools 75
metallurgy 74–75, 81, 86
metalwork 28, 55
finds 36–37
Mexico 81
Middle Ages 82–83
Middle East 70, 72
migration 62–63
Minoan culture 14, 33, 78, 79, 81
Modern Era 83
da Molina, Cristóbal 113
Mongols 78
monument protection 119
monuments 73
Morocco 56
Morris, William 118
mummies 16
mummification 45
Museum of London 49
museums 122, 123
musical instruments 65

Native Americans 24, 63,
107, 108
Native Canadians 21
Nautical Archaeological Society
97

Neanderthals 22, 35, 46, 57, 59, 61
  burials 45, 58, 65
Near East 47, 50, 86
Nebra Sky Disc 112
needles 64
Neolithic 15, 23, 29, 43, 54, 55, 66, 67, 70–72, 78, 79, 90–91
Netherlands 25
New World 55, 71, 113
Nikitin, Sergei 104
Nile 12, 71, 84, 93
nomadic peoples 87
North America
  Clovis culture 23
  Vikings 21
North Sea 67, 68
Norway 21, 68

O'Connor, Sue 63
ochre 45, 65
Ohalo II, Israel 70, 71
Old World 55, 113
Olduvai Gorge, Tanzania 25, 59, 84
Olmecs 54, 80, 81, 88
Olympic Games 81
optically stimulated luminescence (OSL) dating 25
ornament 64–65

Pakistan 80, 86
Palaeolithic 54, 58–59, 64, 65, 182, 67
Papua New Guinea 46, 67
Peking Man 46, 57, 61
Persia 78, 86
Peru 89, 113
Petrie, Sir Flinders 30, 31
petrological analysis 99
Phillips, Philip 55
Phoenicians 81
photoluminescence (PL) dating 25
pits 13, 20–21, 29
Pleistocene 58, 66
Plutarch 104

pollen 32–33, 62
Pompeii 16, 17, 51
populations 46–47
Port of Theodosius 50–51
post holes 16
  Mesolithic 67
post-excavation 9, 10–11
potassium-argon dating 25, 57
pottery 38–39
  dating evidence 14–15
  egg-shell pottery 80
  food preparation 40–41
public archaeology 117
publication 48–49
Pugin, Augustus 114–115
Pulak, Dr Cemal 50
pyramids 45, 80, 84, 119

Qin Shi Huang 45, 86–87
Qinghai-Tibetan Plateau 34–35
Quarry of the Ancestors, Canada 35

Radford, Ralegh 39
railways 95
reading 123
Reck, Hans 59
Reiter, Christian 103
religion 67, 82–83
Renaissance 83
residual material 15
ritual 67, 91
robbing 15
rock art 64, 79
Rodwell, Warwick 99
Roman Britain 15, 17, 25
  Hadrian's Wall 42–43
Roman Germany 25, 27
Romani 87, 109
Romans 14, 15, 16, 37, 45, 47, 51, 193, 78, 82, 83
Ruskin, John 118
Russia 64, 65, 67, 104

Saint Benedict 44–45
salt 41
sampling strategy 108–109
sampling techniques 68
Saunders, Nicholas 107
Scandinavia 69
scatters 34–35
Scotland 42, 47, 67, 69, 73
sculpture 81, 83
Scythians 10
sea levels 62, 66, 69

seriation 30–31
Sheffield 95
shells 64, 65
Shinto 82
Siberian land bridge 23, 34
silver 15
site archive 48–49
site features 13
site reports 10, 48, 49
Skara Brae, Orkney 53, 73
slave trade 83, 85
Slovenia 65
societies 121
Spain 47, 73, 83, 89, 113
specialisms 93
specialists 10, 26, 28–29
  buildings 100–101
specialization 75
standing stones 75
Star Carr, Yorkshire 67, 69
Stone Age 54, 55, 58–59, 78
stone circles 45
Stonehenge 19, 20–21, 37, 53, 67, 78, 79, 80, 112, 113
stratigraphy 12–13, 17, 27, 56
  carbon-14 dating 20–21
  churches 98
structuralism 109
Sumatra 62
Sumerians 79, 81
Sweden 70
Syria 71, 72, 81

Tacitus 27
Tanzania 25, 59
Tasmania 67
taxonomy 26
team work 11
teeth 42, 43, 46
television 117, 123
Tell Brak 81
Tell es Sa'idiyeh, Jordan 43
temples 45
Teotihuacán 88, 89
terminus ante quem 17
terminus post quem 16
terracotta warriors 45, 86
Theodosius 50
Thera 33, 51
thermoluminescence (TL) dating 25, 38
Thom, Alexander 112
Thucydides 47, 53
Tigris 12, 71, 80
Tintagel, Cornwall 39

Tutankhamun 45, 84, 104–105
typologies 26–27, 28–29, 37

Uganda 59
Ukraine 67
Underwater sites 96–97
UNESCO 94, 119
Ur 79, 80
Urns 11, 37, 55
Uruk 79, 80, 81
Ussher, James 56

Valdivia culture 80–81
Valley of the Kings, Egypt 53, 84
Vietnam 87
Vikings 21, 47
Vinland 21
Virgil Aeneid 82
volcanic eruptions 17, 24, 25, 149, 51
volunteers 117, 120, 121

Wales 47, 69
warfare 77, 81, 89
  battlefield archaeology 106–107
Wawruch, Dr Andreas 103
weapons 75, 77
websites 49, 68, 95, 97, 101, 103, 120, 121, 122, 123
West Bank 71
wheels 80, 81
wood 55
World Heritage Sites 94, 119
World War I 106, 107
World War II 106, 107
wrecks 97
writing 79, 86

X-raying 36

Yorkshire 49, 67

Zambia 65
Zimbabwe 85
zooarchaeologists 102
Zoroastrianism 198